About the Editors

DOROTHY HAMILTON founded The French Culinary Institute in 1984. Her career in vocational education and her reputation for innovative programs in gastronomy have resulted in numerous accolades and tributes. Hamilton has also received the coveted Silver Spoon Award from *Food Arts* magazine, recognizing her as a leader in the American restaurant community. Hamilton is chairwoman emerita for life of the American Institute of Wine and Food and has served on the advisory boards of many organizations, including the National Association of Trade and Technical Schools, the International Association of Women Chefs and Restaurateurs, and the U.S. Department of Education. She is also chairwoman of the Board of Trustees for the James Beard Foundation.

PATRIC KUH is the restaurant critic for *Los Angeles Magazine* and author of *The Last Days of Haute Cuisine: The Coming of Age of American Restaurants*, which won the 2002 James Beard Award for writing on food. His articles have appeared in *Gourmet, Bon Appetit, Food & Wine, Esquire*, the *Los Angeles Times, San Francisco* magazine, and Salon.com. His essays have appeared in *Best American Food Writing* over the last few years. Patric spent ten years as a chef in France, New York, and California. He lives in Los Angeles.

Chef's Story

Also by Patric Kuh

The Last Days of Haute Cuisine

27 Chefs
Talk About
What Got
Them into
the Kitchen

Chef's Story

Edited by
Dorothy Hamilton
and Patric Kuh

Photographs by
Matthew Septimus

AN ECCO BOOK

HARPER PERENNIAL

NEW YORK • LONDON • TORONTO • SYDNEY • NEW DELHI • AUCKLAND

HARPER ● PERENNIAL

A hardcover edition of this book was published in 2007 by Ecco, an imprint of Harper-Collins Publishers.

CHEF'S STORY. Copyright © 2007 by Soho Culinary Productions, LLC. All rights reserved. Printed in the United States of America. No part of this book may be used or reproduced in any manner whatsoever without written permission except in the case of brief quotations embodied in critical articles and reviews. For information address HarperCollins Publishers, 10 East 53rd Street, New York, NY 10022.

HarperCollins books may be purchased for educational, business, or sales promotional use. For information please write: Special Markets Department, HarperCollins Publishers, 10 East 53rd Street, New York, NY 10022.

FIRST HARPER PERENNIAL EDITION PUBLISHED 2008.

Designed by Jessica Shatan Heslin
Photographs by Matthew Septimus

Library of Congress Cataloging-in-Publication Data is available upon request.

ISBN 978-0-06-124123-9 (pbk.)

08 09 10 11 12 ID/RRD 10 9 8 7 6 5 4 3 2 1

Acknowledgments

I don't know how many people actually read book acknowledgments. I started to read them years ago when I wrote a preface to one of The French Culinary Institute's books. I realized then how many people it takes to make a book—it takes a village. So please bear with me because this book and this show took almost a town.

First and foremost, I thank my lucky stars that my coauthor, Patric Kuh, decided to take on this project. Although his voice is muted by those of the twenty-seven chefs, his brilliant editing incisively bares the soul of each of these masters. Matthew Septimus's photographs are sensational. They almost tell the story without the words. A big thank-you to Dan Halpern at Ecco, who believed in the book, and our editor, Emily Takoudes, for making it happen overnight. Kim Witherspoon is the best agent in the business. Period. And Ken Swezey was invaluable for his legal insights.

Chef's Story would not have made it to television if my talented, hard-charging husband, Doug, did not take the lead. He always thought the show was a great idea, but once it began to take form, he became its biggest advocate, adviser, and producer.

We must start at the beginning and thank all those who made the television show possible. My first thanks to Marc Navarre, the CEO of All-Clad, who was the first sponsor to believe in the project. If All-Clad did not share our vision for *Chef's Story*, I think that this project would still be a dream. Many thanks also to Lisa Callaghan and Melissa Palmer, who made sure that our chefs worked with the very best equipment available.

This is a story with many fathers, not least of whom is John Servidio. John was the producer of *Inside the Actors Studio* and came to me with the idea for *Chef's Story* in 2003. His instincts were fabulous not to mention his technical skills (and he has an Emmy or two to prove it!).

Susie Heller, Harry Bernstein, and Full Plate Media brought their television savvy and food integrity to the programming. Their associate Amy Vogler is a one-woman wonder. Twenty-seven perfectionists left our set impressed with their level of culinary support and expertise. Accolades go to the talented chef David Shalleck, who shopped and held forth in the back kitchens. We were blessed to have the gentle giant Bruce Francini as our director. He could make a blood sausage look good. The crew that worked under him managed to be both technically brilliant and a lot of fun. Kudos to Paul Swensen, our brilliant editor. Wonderful Susan Gammie led me on the fashion search for the challenging twenty-seven "tops," and Roger Mooney transformed our amphitheater into a dynamic set. My hair and makeup never looked better thanks to Vincent Da Silva of the Gil Ferrer Salon. And the show would not be so smooth if not for the interns—Illana Blumberg, Amanda Cann, Christine Carroll, Andrew Gerdes, Susan Greenberg, Meggin Juraska, Nikki Reiss, Robyn Stern, Baley Walsh, Brooke Weeber.

The show was taped at The French Culinary Institute, where our president, Gary Apito, daily inspires and leads an amazing group of people. Cindy Renzi, Katie McManus, Lee Anne Wong, and Jay Dietershagen kept the amphitheater in as professional a support mode as one could imagine. There are many people at the FCI that made this happen: Robin Cohen, Gwen Korbel, Chris Papagni, Matt Randall and the facilities crew, Erik Murnighan, Holly Moore, Dianne Rossomando, Yannick Guerin, Joshua Campbell, Jim Joseph, Rena Katz, Phil Engert and the faculty and students at the school who allowed us to commandeer the amphitheater for all those weeks. Paula Burns and her hardworking team at Burns Transcription Service rapidly transcribed the interview tapes.

Last but not least, I want to thank my daughter, Olivia, for being the perfect child during those days of grueling taping!

Contents

Preface

How do you tell a chef's story?

About four years ago, John Servidio, a producer of the TV hit *Inside the Actors Studio,* came to my office at The French Culinary Institute. His production company was interested in doing a similar program with chefs. John was not looking for me to host the show, but had come to ask who I thought might be a good interviewer. I gave him a few names but eventually overcame my modesty and suggested myself. As the head of The French Culinary Institute, I had worked for years with master chefs. Not only that, the FCI has been growing them for more than twenty years! I understood chefs and knew that I could ask the right questions. I guess *that* was a good interview, because I got the job.

What a thrill. I now was going to interview twenty-seven of the most fascinating chefs working in America.

I figured there were going to be four groups of viewers for the program: other chefs, wanna-be chefs, foodies, and people who stumbled on the program. I had to make sure that I asked the question that every cook in America was dying to know. I had to bring out each chef's life story and how it had contributed to his or her success. And then, hardest of all, would be having them transcend their trade and reveal their inner chef, giving the public an insight to these extraordinary people who have the stamina of oxen and the souls of artists.

Many people dream of being chefs because they love to cook. It's fun. But professional cooking hardly qualifies as fun. It is way too hard, too demanding, and too competitive. Most of these masters became chefs because there was no alternative. It was a calling, a vocation.

Cooking is a demanding profession that requires patience, long hours, years of apprenticing, and hard, physical work. It is also a nurturing world with tremendous camaraderie. It takes years to become proficient with the necessary skills, and then to be *the* chef, you must be a logistics and human resource manager par excellence. To be a master chef you need to go even further and have a special talent. You must have an understanding of food and its possibilities that most of us cannot fathom. You need to be open to many influences but also maintain your identity. And most of all you need to cook with love.

Some people might approach *Chef's Story* with the idea that chefs are arrogant, screaming maniacs in their kitchens. That is a caricature. You will find that our featured chefs are as nuanced as any artist, as business minded as any entrepreneur, and as hardworking as any coal miner.

Each chef's story is different, and each path to greatness was not an easy road. The differences are enormous! Patrick O'Connell never went to cooking school or studied under a great chef (self-inspiring). Tom Colicchio worked for fast food joints (not inspiring). Suzanne Goin traveled the three-star Michelin gastronomic route in Europe with her parents as a teenager (awe-inspiring).

Are there similarities? Yes. Good chefs never stop learning. Jean-Georges Vongerichten went to business school in between being executive chef at the four-star Lafayette and opening the first place of his own, JoJo. David Bouley travels the world incessantly and has penetrated the innermost circles of master chefs in Japan. The éminence grise André Soltner says he looks to learn something new every day.

It is also no surprise that chefs today are business people. To listen to Charlie Palmer and hear the growth of his "empire," you realize that cooking is not his only strength. We get an insight from Thomas Keller on his rugged climb to being the first American to receive six stars from the Michelin guide. And Bobby Flay shares the pros and cons of being a star on the Food Network.

There are immigrant stories. Stories of living in occupied France during World War II. Spiritual stories. Stories of balancing professional and personal lives. Stories of sacrifice.

It's all here.

We are so lucky that Patric Kuh took on the challenge of writing this book. A former cook himself, he gets it. He sat through each taping, and in his beautiful style captured it for us on the ensuing pages. Matthew Septimus's photography transcended the show. We scratched the idea of doing our planned "B" roll filming at the chefs' restaurants in favor of Matthew's shooting photo essays at their establishments.

What a show! What an experience. What a privilege. *Chef's Story* provides a unique insight into this wonderful profession and these very talented individuals.

DOROTHY HAMILTON

Chef's
Story

José
Andrés

The Spanish-born culinary innovator José Andrés has seven restaurants in the Washington, D.C., area. He has been praised by the *New York Times* as the "boy wonder of culinary Washington" and was named Chef of the Year by *Bon Appétit*. His talent was recognized early on in his career, when he was nominated for the James Beard Rising Star Chef of the Year Award and won the Best Chef Mid-Atlantic. He started his career at El Bulli and continued his rise at Café Atlántico, Oyamel, Zaytinya, and Jaleo, eventually opening two other Jaleos. Most recently, Andrés opened Minibar, his innovative six-seat restaurant within a restaurant. He recently published his first cookbook, *Tapas*.

I grew up in a little town, a half hour from Barcelona. The population was about five hundred people and ninety percent of them were farmers. We had lots of fruits and vegetables, but we had amazing cherry trees. In May and June, when the trees were loaded with fruit, my friends and I had a very curious kind of competition. We would eat the cherries off the tree without separating the pit from the stem or the stem from the branch. The lower branches of these trees would be nothing more than hanging pits. The neck movements required for this were far beyond anything that yoga has devised. I was an expert.

My parents were both nurses, and they cooked at home for me— since in those days, in the early seventies in Spain, there wasn't much money, and most restaurants were out of the question. My father really loved to cook on weekends, out in the countryside. He would make a big paella on an open fire for friends and family. By the time I was in my early teens, I was put in charge of the fire. I would gather the wood—often orange tree wood but other kinds also—and build the fire and spread out the embers, which is very important because too high a heat can ruin a paella. If I even put a finger near where he was preparing the food he would say, "No. You're in charge of the fire." At a certain stage I got upset that this was all I was allowed to do. He said, "José, don't you understand? I was giving you the most important task. If you control the fire you, too, will make a good paella one day."

I was very interested in cooking, and I was helping at home all the time. My mother would be in the kitchen peeling some red peppers that she would roast, and she would make this kind of nice stew with garlic and sherry vinegar and oil. I would help peel. But in Spain we picked up a fascination with food literally by breathing; it was in the air. In the mornings it was the churros frying in huge vats of oil that would be deposited still piping hot on newspaper and sprinkled with sugar. At lunch the predominant smell of the street was olive oil heated for frying. Most women didn't work outside the home in those days, and men always came home in the middle of the day. The streets, alleys, and stairwells of any town had a certain regional nuance. A long-simmered *cocido* full of chickpeas and chorizo in the interior, a *fabada* Asturiana in the northern region of Asturias; in Andalucia, there'd be lots of fried fish.

In Barcelona we had a veritable codfish culture; we didn't just have stores that specialized in salt cod, we had stores that specialized in how they desalted it. There's more than one school of thought on that subject. After all, when you put a fillet of salt cod in water, in the process of osmosis you are taking away molecules that are very important for the flavor. If you keep on taking away water and putting in fresh water you are harming the flavor. Barcelona is a city that understands that. The difference between the stores is how much water they take out and how long the desalting process lasts. One sells cod that has spent one day in water, another two days, another three days but with only half of the original water replaced.

My father liked to buy the cod still half salted and to finish the process himself. I loved that flavor, and when no one was around I often slipped a little morsel in my mouth. Unfortunately when you broke off a piece it was very obvious, and my father always would sigh. "José, did you eat it again? Could you cut it and not eat it with your fingers?"

He liked to cook it very simply, just fry it gently in a batter of flour and egg. Salt cod is already cooked by the salt; you need only warm it to make it perfect, magical to the palate. But if you cook it harshly, by searing or boiling, it loses its natural gelatin and becomes dry and hard. Everyone in Barcelona understands this, too. The charm of cod consumption in Barcelona is that there is the bond of obsessiveness that links purveyor and consumer.

So did cooking click for me, or did I just give in? I don't think I can answer that. The patterns of life are perceived only in hindsight.

3

I was surrounded by food, fascinated by how it was prepared, and it was natural to try and constantly seek out more knowledge. When I was fifteen I worked in a three-person restaurant in a tiny town, and Ferrán Adrià used to come in to eat on his days off. I used to see him through the tiny window in the kitchen. He was the chef of the best restaurant in town, and though he wasn't yet famous in the outside world, he was a star to us. At first we thought we had to impress him, but he loved eating simple things, traditional things like garlic shrimp, *gambas al ajillo* or fish cooked *a la plancha*. I would make that dish for him. A year later, by the time I was a student at the famous culinary school Escola de Restauració i Hostalatge de Barcelona and I was privileged to be sent for an internship under Ferrán at El Bulli.

One needs to be proud about the people you learn from. Often they are the unsung heroes. Ferrán is very well known now, but sometimes you learn from people that are not known. As cooks we should always have gratitude for those we learn from; we are the ones who can most honestly proclaim the importance of that individual. I have eternal gratitude to Ferrán. He gave me the vantage point from which to approach cooking. There is nothing a teacher can give that is more valuable.

I remember one particular moment when I realized this. We were making a gelatin of milk for a *bavarois* and there happened to be a pot of hot oil on the stove. He got a piece of what we were making, just as it had begun to set, and he threw it into the hot oil. Well, if you think about it, the gelatin is only going to give body to the milk if it's cold. Everybody is going to tell you that the heat will melt the gelatin and there will be a little explosion because of the water content. Ferrán didn't care. He wanted to see it. Well, there was a little explosion.

His action didn't result in an unbelievable new dessert called deep-fried *bavarois,* but in something much more important: the proof of a hypothesis. There is a culinary logic, but if we never test it we are missing very important information. He did it because doing it was the only way to know. What Ferrán does at his brilliantly inventive restaurant, El Bulli, is remind us cooks that we need to keep testing things on our own.

I was in the navy for my military service. I wanted to go into this boat called *Juan Sebastián del Cano,* which is a four-mast sailing boat with a crew of three hundred. I'd first seen that boat when I was eight and it had visited Barcelona. Ten years later I had the opportunity to do so, but when I requested service on the boat, I was told no. I had already won a couple of little championships and I had worked in good restaurants. "You're going to be the cook of the admiral," they told me. So I started as the cook of the admiral of the fleet in his residence. But two weeks before the ship was to leave port, I couldn't contain myself. I asked to see him and I said, "Admiral, sailing on this boat is the dream of my life." He said, "Okay, you can go, but don't tell my wife." Two days before I left, he told his wife. I'm not sure how he put it, but it must have sounded like, "The cook is leaving, you're not going to have more cooking classes and no more coffee and tea cakes for your friends." She screamed. "What are you doing? The admiral in this house is me!"

It was through the navy that I started to experience the world and see how truly diverse and yet similar food could be. In Abidjan, in the Ivory Coast, I had the traditional *kedjenou,* a deep-flavored stew that I saw prepared from the moment the chicken was killed right in front of me. In Fortaleza, Brazil, I tasted papaya for the first time. It was served

in a tiny restaurant, more like a bar, and they split the papaya and scooped out the seeds and they served it with half a lime and a spoon. That tropical magnificence was something I had never experienced before.

By the time we got to Pensacola, I was looking forward to American food but I didn't know what to expect. Hot dogs, milkshakes, and fries—I knew those. What would be the moment of surprise in this huge country? The fact that we were in Pensacola as part of a celebration commemorating all the countries that had conquered Pensacola was already something of a surprise. But soon after arriving, there would be a culinary one. I met a guy named Jerry who owned a restaurant, and when he found out I was a cook, he took me there. The first thing he gave me was a soft-shell crab. That was a discovery. I said, "Oh, it's very difficult to peel this crab." "José," he said, "you eat it all." I did, and it was delicious. Things are only obvious to people who know it.

On that trip we would also sail to Norfolk, Virginia, and eventually we sailed into New York Harbor, a fascinating moment when you round a piece of land and the city suddenly opens up before you. All it took was shore leave and ten minutes on the sidewalks of New York to know I was coming back to America. Unfortunately, I eventually returned to work at a restaurant that failed. There were a few Spanish restaurants that opened around 1992, the year of the Olympics in Barcelona, and an outfit I worked for owned several of them. In Washington they had La Taverna del Lavadero, and in New York, El Dorado Petit and Paradis Barcelona—all of them were closed five years later. The reviews were good, but the main problem was they tried to reinvent Spanish cooking in America trying to think what Americans would like. As a Spanish cook, a dish like chicken and grapefruit can certainly make you scratch your head. If you can make duck with oranges why not chicken with grapefruit? Maybe it's good; but it's definitely not Spanish.

Spanish cooking has a great simplicity. That has always been the case. We always have had an aesthetic ideal. The still lifes you might see in the Prado museum in Madrid might contain only a crusty loaf of bread and a bottle of wine; a domestic scene might be an old lady frying an egg in a terracotta pot. After the civil war in the 1930s there was also a true moment of hunger that the entire country lived through and that marked an entire generation. There is also a fascinating sociological interpretation for our long tradition of pork products that maintains that eating pork in public was a means of establishing one was Christian in the centuries in Spain when it was very dangerous not to be. Something austere in the Spanish personality craves the simple product while at the same time elevating it to its most refined state. The salt cod of my childhood is but one example. The *jamon* Iberico that today we are finally being allowed to import into the U.S. is another example. This ham comes from semi-wild black-footed pigs that are allowed to forage in chestnut forests for several months. Their hind legs are cured for up to three years, and the resulting ham is best cut very thinly because the temperature at which the fat melts and the temperature of our mouths are almost identical. It should practi-

Chef's Story José Andrés

7

cally dissolve in the mouth. *Caramba!* This is a molecular tapa, and it doesn't even come from El Bulli.

This is the kind of food that I wanted to make when I left New York for Washington. I was encouraged to do so by precisely one of those unsung heroes that we have in our profession. He was a Spaniard, and he had come to this country with nothing and was chef and co-owner of El Cid, a restaurant on Fifteenth Street between Eighth and Ninth avenues. His name was Clemente Bocos, and I am proud to write his name here. Before I moved to Washington he said, "José, do whatever you want. You are talented and you know the flavors. You are adapting very well to America but be truthful to the flavors of the country you come from. Don't try to reinvent traditional Spanish cooking, just respect it. In America they can like many things, but it needs to be good."

Those words could be inscribed over the door at Jaleo. From when we opened the first one, in 1993, it has been a platform for what I feel is best about Spain. For me, as important as the food is the social aspect of sharing. That is a Spanish moment. That is exactly what I try to do. It's a restaurant where the average check doesn't matter. It's fine if they eat one tapa and one sherry or one beer. I don't need them to be there three hours; I just need this moment of attention to Spanish cooking.

What I feel it offers is more than just fantastic ingredients like *pimentón* or *jamon* Iberico, but a point of view on food that does not derive from abundance. Often in this country I've found that when something is good you get a lot of it, as if that will make it better. In cooking that has a more austere perspective, the approach is different. When something is good you get very little, but you make it last and make it count.

On the other extreme we have a minibar in which we can only do six people (or twelve, with two seatings per night). This is my curious side, the one that is about a different tradition, the one of asking questions. We do twelve customers per night, and meals can stretch to thirty-five tiny courses. What I seek to do is take a look at the ingredients, nicks and all. That may be trying to figure out everything from if we can make sauterne cotton candy (the answer is yes) to the gastronomic uses for the pulp of pips at the center of a tomato. These are full of flavor, fascinating, and gelatinous, and yet the passed-down rules of haute cuisine demanded we get rid of them? Why? Because someone said they are unbecoming? Because centuries ago some chef saw that a farmhouse salad contained pits and we don't want to be like them? There are entire social dimensions behind how we treat a tomato, what we keep and what we throw out.

I operate between those two poles. I am a man who can remember the smells of the stairwells of his childhood, a man for whom the first taste of a papaya opened up a dimension of flavor that had been unknown before. I understand the need for tradition and I am fascinated by the process of constantly reaching further beyond what we already know. Food allows us to do that, to literally broaden our world. Once I'd never heard of pancakes; now on weekend mornings I'm happily making them for my three daughters. Once I tried to peel the shell of softshell crabs, now I know you eat them whole.

Dan Barber

Dan Barber is the man behind Blue Hill in New York City and Blue Hill at Stone Barns, in Pocantico, New York, both acclaimed for locally grown and seasonal produce. He has been named by *Bon Appétit* part of the "next generation of great chefs" and by *Food & Wine* as one of the "best new chefs." In 2006 he was awarded the James Beard Foundation Award for Best Chef, New York City.

I graduated from school wanting to write about food. It's been a real process along the way in terms of simultaneously becoming a better chef and a leader, but also learning about this whole other world of agriculture and where our food really comes from. And a lot of that has just been discovery. It's like, holy mackerel! We're eating meat from cows that don't eat grass. That's pretty incredible. Those are the things people don't know anything about. So my education has both been learning about sustainable agriculture, but also, how do I communicate this to the average diner who couldn't care less that cows don't eat grass? They want their steak and they want their chardonnay, and they want to leave. And so I feel like I end up becoming quite preachy, and I don't want to be. But the older I get, the less patience I have to be skirting around the issues.

I would get rid of the word *organic* altogether. We have a restaurant, Blue Hill at Stone Barns, on a farm thirty miles outside New York. The farm, called Stone Barns Center for Food and Agriculture, has a herd of Dorset Cross sheep, eight hundred laying hens that produce a thousand dozen eggs a month and a hundred and fifty broilers, twenty acres of pasture, twenty-three thousand contiguous feet of organic land, and a herd of Berkshire pigs who like to sit in the shade trees out back. I like guests to take the time and walk around before dinner and see what is happening on the farm. But often their first question is, "Are you organic?" "Are your pigs organic?" I want them to ask me, "What do your pigs eat?" But when they look at the chickens and look at the eggs, the big question is, "Are your eggs organic?" I want to look at them and say, "Our chickens are organic but they also eat grass."

The public wants easy answers and so do I, and organic/non-organic makes for a very tidy evil/non-evil narrative. The organic question, however, is very complex. There are ways of growing organic that are good for the soil and ways that completely deplete it. A chicken may be in a ten-thousand-bird shed eating corn all its life, but it is organic. For chefs, it is particularly important because of the quantities of produce we need. It is pretty much impossible to grow organic strawberries in the Northeast, certainly in a volume to sustain a restaurant. It's just plain silly to ship them from California—a single basket uses up a ton of fossil fuel calories in refrigeration and transportation just so you can put the word *organic* on your dessert menu. I would much rather have a relationship with a local farmer who I know will spray only when conditions make it absolutely necessary.

These are the issues that are important to me. So if people are going to say I sound haughty and arrogant and elitist, well, I've stopped counting the number of times I have heard those criticisms. What is important is that *organic* is more than a word to slap on packaging or on a menu. It comes from *organism*; it means "the whole." There are three legs to it. It's not just how it's farmed, but who is farming it and, very important, where is it coming from? Who is growing your food? What community is growing it for you? That's the name of the game.

I grew up on the Upper East Side of Manhattan, but I spent a lot of time on my grandmother's farm in the Berkshires, in Massachusetts. It is called Blue Hill Farm. It was a working farm, and my grandmother raised cattle. I learned about food and agriculture there. My grandmother's cooking philosophy was that food tastes better when you're hungry. So she always made me wait. She'd say dinner was ready, and then I'd wait forty-five minutes. But the food always tasted better. And her cooking wasn't that great, so she needed the help.

My grandmother and I both read Eliot Coleman. He has a farm called the Four Seasons Farm, in Maine, and he has a great ability to farm, and an equal ability to write about what he is doing. I was reading his books while I was in college because I was interested in how to grow vegetables at Blue Hill and how we could use the farm with some kind of cooking and community component. My grandmother was interested in his approach to farming for more basic reasons, like how do we keep this going financially? Although I'd read books like *Diet for a Small Planet* and *Silent Spring,* Eliot was the one who was writing about growing vegetables in the Northeast year-round. He said that we could grow vegetables in the middle of winter even at Blue Hill Farm.

In a way I was thinking about Stone Barns long before I was introduced to the farm. The path to making Stone Barns a reality would be a long one. First I became a chef. My mentors in terms of cooking have been many. Alain Sailhac at the French Culinary Institute first taught me that being a chef is not just how you cook but how you behave. Michel Rostang took me in when I knew very little and gave me a sense of Provence. Joe Miller's restaurant in Venice, California, was where I had my first hard-core-line position. I had cooked at a bunch of different restaurants but never with that intensity. He made me delight in the sheer athleticism of cooking and taught me how you constantly have to adapt. David Bouley was like a finishing school where the passion and sheer energy and force of will required rubbed off on me.

My brother, David, and his wife, Laureen, and I opened Blue Hill in 2000, seven years after I graduated from the FCI. We got some good reviews early, but I won't say it was easy. It was really difficult, because we were in a location that's off the beaten track there. Washington Place is one street that no one could find, although that ended up working to our advantage, because people showed up hungrier. But we were also really lucky with the space. We appeared about the same time as big New York restaurants like Eleven Madison Park and Tabla—real experience restaurants.

We also arrived before the deluge of Lower East Side restaurants. We created a restaurant that was cavernous and off the track, and I feel that added to our success, because people came in and walked down the steps from the street and they literally had to bow their heads at the low door. With such an approach they didn't know what to expect. There was paper on the tables, the glassware wasn't perfect, but when they tasted the food, I think it met, even exceeded, their expectations. That is so rare for us in this world, whether it's with movies or anything else in our life. Normally in New York restaurants your expectation level is the sky, and the food is usually wonderful, but if it falls short, it feels depressing. With us, it helped fund our success.

David Rockefeller, along with his aid, James Ford, ate at Blue Hill several times. I think they both loved the food. I believe that Mr. Rockefeller liked the place, and he really liked the family aspect of it. My brother's involved in the business, my sister-in-law designed the restaurants, and our sister is our lawyer. Mr. Rockefeller was looking to do something with a few stone barns that his father built at the turn of the century. John D. Rockefeller, Jr., wanted his children and grandchildren to milk their own cows—that was the original purpose of the barns.

It's pretty valuable land up in Westchester County, but Rockefeller didn't want to see just houses built on the land. He and Ford basically said, "This is an open book. Let's talk about doing a project." I didn't want to open just another restaurant, but one that had a true connection to this very special space. That ended up really resonating with him.

The center is magnificent. There's eye candy all around. It's real Rockefeller largesse in that sense, but not ostentatious at all. The gorgeous old stone barns are where the restaurant and the education center are located. We have over a hundred children a week using the education center, plus we have a lively summer camp. The fact that Blue Hill at Stone Barns sits in the middle of all this land is a rare opportunity to engage in a kind of food/agriculture system that we all want. If you show up to Stone Barns, plop yourself down to eat, and then you leave, it's probably like most other restaurants. But if you give yourself the time to walk around the vegetables and the gardens and see the animals and then sit down to a meal, it's hard to duplicate. You can order a tomato salad in August and look out on a field of growing tomatoes, and all of a sudden it's the best tomato salad you've ever tasted. So I'm grateful to Mr. Rockefeller and to Stone Barns, because together they have made me a better chef in many different respects.

One of the big misconceptions is that Mr. Rockefeller is subsidizing the center. People think I'm the luckiest chef in the world and that we get free food. Sometimes when he's walking by he'll say, "Hiya, partner," which is kind of nice to hear; but in fact, Mr. Rockefeller provided the initial funding for the project and said, "Thank you very much for being involved. Now it's up to you to make it work." And so the farm needs to make a profit. I have this split personality, because I'm also creative director of the center. So I want to make sure the idea works. If the farm makes money, then I've also got to attend to our own food costs and make sure that we can pay the rent that also helps support the farm and the education center. So all day I'm considering these issues.

Take the carrots, for example. I could get them from one hundred miles north. I wouldn't even have to go into the industrial-organic food chain and I could pay thirty percent less for carrots that are grown in a similar way. It's really ironic when you think about it. I'm staring at a field of carrots that are similar to those that I can buy from one hundred miles away for thirty percent cheaper, and I could buy for fifty percent cheaper from Mexico. Organic carrots that I could get deliv-

ered at the door at seven the next morning beautifully boxed and perfect looking. They may not be the greatest carrots but they'd be fifty percent cheaper and they'd be organic. So there's this conundrum. In fact, the real irony is that my food costs—last month they were thirty-eight percent—would get most chefs fired. But to support the farm, to support the center and its mission, I have to pay fair market value for a carrot grown in the middle of Westchester County.

Those aren't the only hard decisions. Another is that I really mean *seasonal*. There are transition seasons when nothing has come in yet. In the early spring every restaurant menu in New York has asparagus, peas, ramps, fiddlehead ferns, tomatoes, everything, and mine reads *dull, dull, dull*—and I've got the farm!

Another one is that we don't serve beef. I used to have beef all over the menu, but the more I learn about how cows are being raised,

I can't support it. I'm really not this neurotic guy; okay, I am neurotic but I don't want to become less so on this issue. Learning about the conventional ways in which cattle are raised makes me just not want to eat steak. Today, in the massive feedlots in the Midwest and West they're constantly trying to speed up the rate in which cattle go from calving weight to slaughter weight, and they do it by pumping them with corn and antibiotics. Cows are ruminants; they're not even supposed to eat corn. That's without even getting into the environmental effects of the leaching and runoff from the manure lakes in these feedlots.

It's the same argument of philosophical logic versus economic logic with my carrots. The economic logic is to get a cow to go through the system as quickly as possible. The philosophical argument demands that you are at least aware of what that entails. It gets awfully political; but food is political. Food choices are political, right? And as chefs we have a responsibility, at least a small responsibility, to purchase food that's good for ourselves, good for our diners, good for our children, and good for our neighborhoods. We have huge buying power and huge influence, and the decisions we make have effects on how our communities function.

I'm very conscious of wanting the restaurant to seem modern. You go to Stone Barns and we have modern glassware and there's beautiful tableware and linens, and yet you feel like you are in a barn. So you have the modernity, the modern aspects of life, which I feel are important. They make you feel of the moment. I don't want to be a throwback to a hundred years ago and some kind of museum of special food. We're not cooking by the fire, we've even heard of sous vide.

One of my challenges as a chef is that the more beautiful the produce, the less I want to do to it. Carrots are something near and dear to my heart. We have Napoli carrots, which are particularly sweet in the winter, and when there's a nice cold snap they just taste as sweet as they can possibly taste. Well, maybe I'll just want to shred them. I make a lemon vinaigrette by taking tons of lemon skins and infusing it in olive oil and I mix it with a little lemon juice and mustard to make an emulsion. I use it a lot. It finishes all the vegetables and the salads because I feel it picks things up without the acidity that makes you pucker. Well, a salad like that is pretty understated. Sometimes I think people leave and say, "What's the big deal? I'm not in Nirvana."

The more nuanced you are the more you're walking a tightrope, because a lot of people just won't get it. And that's not to place the blame on them. People's lives are so harried. They've got the kids and they've got this and that; they come for the meal and want to be blown away. And why shouldn't they be?

What I find really helps is getting the staff involved in communicating the story of the vegetables. You have to give information to the waiters, and they can take it from there. I don't want to be controlling the words. The best waiters are good storytellers. If you give them the information, they know what to do.

Last winter I was disappointed that no one was walking around the property before the meal, so I created this position of vegetable runners. They're like our diplomats. They leave the kitchen with a tray of all the different types of salads and greens, mostly from the greenhouse. They're like nineteen years old, really handsome, really articulate guys and they say things like, "Here's today's harvest. I just wanted you to see this green and this green and this green that will be part of your

19

menu." All of a sudden the whole feeling of a meal can change. There's a connection. That's really what I'm trying to do. People go to France and Italy and they say the food was so much better. Fucking A, it's better, man. You're relaxed, there's a connection between where you are and what you're eating and drinking, and you have no phone ringing and no Internet. You're there among it. Well, let's not just get connected in France and Italy; let's get connected in America.

I can get caught up in the daily grind of the restaurant. One of my big regrets is that when I was a twenty-five-year-old line cook I didn't use that time to become more knowledgeable. I really don't have the luxury of time right now. I don't have time to follow up on all the things I find interesting. I have to put blinders on during the day. I live on Eleventh Street in Manhattan, so I'm firmly settled in New York. I take the produce from Stone Barns down to New York around 12:30 a.m., and so I get in around 1:30 a.m., and it's a long, really long day. And we're open seven days a week. Sometimes I think, "Oh, my God, I'm never going to rest."

But we are constructing a model. One that I hope will show that you don't need proximity to New York to do it. You could have the philosophy of Blue Hill at Stone Barns and Stone Barns Center for Food and Agriculture in Topeka, Kansas. As long as you have a farmer who likes good food and has a connection to a restaurant that wants to support the farm, and there's a school system that will bring in an educational component, then the conditions are all there. We're running out of time. We really are. The middle- and small-size farms are in real trouble in this country. So would Stone Barns exist in North Dakota the way it looks now? No, of course not. And in Kansas it would look different, too. They each have their own sense of place. But you don't need eighty acres in Westchester to connect a farmer, a chef, and an educator. So I'm very hopeful about Stone Barns. If we can be successful on our own and popularize this notion I'm really hopeful that people around the country will see its wisdom. They already have. It's not like we're starting a revolution. It's there already.

Lidia Bastianich

Born in Pola, Istria, the meeting point of Italy and the former Yugoslavia, Lidia Matticchio Bastianich is known as the first lady of Italian cuisine and restaurants in the United States. She has established herself as a TV personality with her shows *Lidia's Italian-American Kitchen* and *Lidia's Italian Table*, each with corresponding cookbooks. In addition to her own line of pasta sauces, she owns several restaurants in New York City, including Felidia and Del Posto, as well as the acclaimed eatery Becco. She has recently opened Lidia's Kansas City and Lidia's Pittsburgh.

People talk about their food memories. My first American food memories are of the Jell-O and grapefruit sold at the Horn & Hardart, in New York City. It was across the street from the hotel where we first lived when we landed in the United States. The place was an Automat, as many things as possible were automated. You entered through revolving doors and on the right there were cubicles like little beehives, with doors that would open and you would put in a nickel or a dime and it would release the door. It could contain a sandwich or a humongous slice of cake, but for us it was always a cup of Jell-O or a cut grapefruit, neither one of which we'd ever tasted before.

In my hometown in Italy (now Croatia), Pola, things were different. There, food revolved around the courtyard of the houses, not Automats on busy city streets. When the bean pods on the plants were mature and just beginning to dehydrate, people would pluck the whole plant, shake out the dirt from the roots, invert the plant, and hang it on a clothesline with pins so it would dry under the sun. When they were dry we'd put sackcloth on the ground and take the pods off and we would sit around the cloth and shell them. Then the kids would hold two sides of cloth and we would toss them in the air, and the wind would blow away everything but the beans, which we would save. We did that with *ceci,* too, and with corn for the animals.

To get the butcher for the ritual of the pig slaughter, the whole town would get together and arrange a date. It was like making an appointment for the doctor to visit. He would go to each courtyard and help each family slaughter their pig, always with the help of several men, because it takes strength to hold a pig down. Then he would butcher it, and the family would work on the curing of the prosciutto and the bacon slabs, the making of sausages, blood sausages, *musetto,* pickled feet—not a morsel wasted. He would cut out the *prosciutti* for the prosciutto. He would cut out the ribs, the bacon slab; then the family would be left with curing all the pieces, and we kids would help out. I remember rubbing salt into certain cuts and making blood sausage.

Pola, however, was to become Pula. That part of the Istrian peninsula was annexed by Yugoslavia, and today it is part of Croatia. The ethnic Italians had the option to leave and go back to Italy. My mother did file, as she was ready to go, but she became pregnant, so she decided to stay at home, especially since her mother was there. And once the iron curtain went down, everything changed. You became the nationality of the occupiers. You couldn't speak Italian or practice your religion, although in border situations one always speaks more than one language, and we spoke Croatian as well.

We finally decided to leave. I remember it was evening when we left, and my grandmother and grandfather and father were at the train station. My father was going to stay behind and would try and join us later. Nobody told us, because children talk, but I sensed something. I recall thinking, why is everyone so upset? We were supposed to be going for a vacation, to visit the part of our family that remained in Italy. Our roots were sort of yanked out from under us. As children we didn't know that we were not going to return. So I didn't say goodbye to my grandmother and I didn't say goodbye to my friends.

We got to Trieste, and a few weeks later my father got out. I remember the night he got to us and he hadn't shaved or slept in days. At that point we were without a nationality. We could have stayed in Italy to get back our Italian nationality, but my parents assessed the situation and, in the aftermath of the war, said, "Let's move on," as we had no passports and were in limbo. They were essentially looking for a country, for a place that would take them.

The Catholic Charities brought us to New York and found us the hotel room and later our first home and a job for my father in America. We couldn't cook at the hotel, so we had to eat everything out. The Horn & Hardart was across the street from the hotel, but we first ate bananas, milk, and bread that we bought at a market. Every Monday we would meet the social worker, and she would ask my mother what we did and how much we ate, and then she would give her money for food. My mother was frugal and would bring the money back and say, "I didn't spend it." This happened so often that the social worker was saying; "Now you have to feed these children. You have to spend the money." So she learned to do that. That's how we finally crossed the street from the hotel and how Jell-O for me came to be a taste memory.

They found us a little house in North Bergen, New Jersey, and then a job for my father, and we stayed there for about nine months. A distant cousin found out that we were here and came looking for us. He was married and had two children and he found us an apartment next to him, in Astoria, Queens. There we were in the milieu of Greek and Italian immigrants, and this is where we began to develop ourselves as Americans-to-be. There were some ethnic ingredients—like there was always olive oil and some dried herbs—but I specifically remember this constant quest of trying to make the right risotto for my father, which he loved, with long-grain rice. The kitchen was more of a cubicle, and we couldn't eat and cook at the same time. Once we were seated, whoever was on that side had to pass the pots, and whoever was on this side had to get to the refrigerator, but it was fun and we were happy.

My mother had been an elementary school teacher back home, and I had always wanted to study. My interest in high school and college was chemistry. I thought I was going to go in that direction. But I met my then husband, seven years my elder, and he was in the restaurant industry. He wanted to open a restaurant; this is what he always wanted to do. His strength was in the front of the house. He was not a chef, but I was willing and excited to help. Even though by then we had our first child, I said, "I'll help you. Let's go ahead." And we found this little thirty-seater in Forest Hills, Queens, and we began.

I had always gravitated toward food and had small jobs as I was growing up. It wasn't my dream to have a restaurant, but I enjoyed it. We hired an Italian American chef and for nine years I worked as his sous-chef. We cooked Italian American food, which is the food of adaptation of all the Italian immigrants of that time. We made veal parmigiana, eggplant parmigiana, veal rollatini, and he executed it very well. But as I gained confidence and expertise, I started inserting my own specialties, the food we cooked and ate at home. The polenta, the gnocchi, the risotto. We didn't even put it on the menu. I would make a big pot of polenta with mushrooms or venison, and when we served the guests their order we would bring a little plate of my specialties for them to taste, listen to their comments, and observe their reaction. We soon realized that those dishes were what they really wanted. They wanted real Italy.

My life then became very complicated. I also had two children, Joseph and Tanya. Everything becomes a question when you're a mother and running a business. Okay, I'll make the gnocchi in the morning. Then it's lunchtime for the kids. Then they come home from school. Do I go pick them up? Do I bring them to the restaurant? Do we have lunch there? Do I bring food from the restaurant and feed them at home? My mother was working as a salesperson in a bakery, and she would get home at three o'clock. Then I would go for the evening to the restaurant. But if we were shorthanded, that system tum-

27

bled. There were plenty of times when my kids would be doing their homework on crates of vegetables. The frustration was immense. I was glad my business was successful, but I felt I wasn't giving enough time to the children.

Who knew about psychology then? You went to your doctor, who supposedly took care of your well-being. So I went to a man who would become very influential in my life, our pediatrician, Dr. Stein. I explained to him how things were and I said, "I feel very guilty, very uneasy about not spending enough time with my children." He looked at me and said, "You know, Lidia, children want happy parents. That's what they want. When the parents are happy and gratified they'll find the time and the family will find a harmony. Children do understand." With those words of wisdom he liberated me, he settled me, putting me at peace. And when I was happy, whenever they were around me, my children were happy as well, and I have a hunch that might have been one of the reasons that made them choose to come and work in the family business.

In fact, I didn't encourage them. I didn't. I pushed them away. From an early age I told them, "This is not what you want to do. Mom has to do this, because she needs to make a living. She has a good time at it. She also needs to pay the college tuition. Your grandmother and grandfather sacrificed and left their native lands so we could have a better and a freer future. To validate that, you need to get a good education and you need to create your own profession, whatever you love to do." Joe was actually a political science and theology major at Boston College, and Tanya got her Ph.D. from Oxford, in Renaissance art history. By the time they wanted to go into the family business, they had achieved their goals and developed as mature and responsible professionals, and at this point, when they decided to enter the family business, I was grateful. I had my doubts, though, as working with your own children is always a challenge.

I am very aware that I am part of a greater legacy. My mother and father came here in their forties, with two children, not knowing where they were going, not knowing a word of the language, and they took us because they wanted a future for us. We need to prove that they did the right thing, that we did make a future and we thank them for that. I also feel that I have helped Americans understand the true simplicity of Italian cooking. It wasn't always easy. You didn't just call

29

up for tiny calamari to grill. You had to go down to the fish market on Long Island early in the morning to try and find them. Modesty was the lesson. A dish might have only two ingredients and the water they cooked in, and it could be great.

It's not that I had a plan. But I am very perceptive, and I sensed what people liked and what they wanted. I gave them what they responded to—straightforward food. If you put on a plate something that is honest and full, even thirty years ago, your taste buds told you the truth. So I think my cooking was based on a great security; I may not have been trained as a chef but I always could trust my sensibility. It was a very stable base and point of departure. Because whatever opportunities come, you have to be ready to make that move. You have to be ready professionally, financially, emotionally, and mentally. Every growth in my career—whether it's been restaurants, television, or books—was not something that I had a long-term plan for, but in most cases it was an opportunity that came which I chose to take. I took my time thinking about how I could make it happen and prepared myself for it, then I took the leap. I surrounded myself with people that were experts.

In my case, I built up this validity in this persona, and once you have the validity and the trust of people, then you can really convey a message—provided that it is true, that it is to their benefit, and that it adds to the quality of their life. So it is very precious to me to have the trust of my audience, and I am always concerned that I merit their trust. Food is my medium, and with it I am transporting the Italian culture, the Italian way of life. I feel empowered by that task and I need to be true to that culture. And yet I feel that my reason for cooking goes even deeper than that. I have looked back and said,

"Why are you so connected? Why are you so passionate about what you do?" It's about holding on to something. When I left Istria at age twelve we were people without a country, refugees. I left my grandmother and all of who I was behind, and I wanted to retain that. I did it through food.

Rick Bayless

Originally from Oklahoma City, Rick Bayless established himself as one of the top experts of Mexican cuisine with his instant-classic cookbook *Authentic Mexican* and five other Mexican-themed cookbooks. His two Chicago restaurants, Frontera Grill and Topolobampo, along with his food line, Frontera Foods, have introduced the world to the hidden jewels of Mexican regional specialties. His many achievements were acknowledged when he received the James Beard Foundation Award for America's Best Chef.

I'm fourth generation in a family of food people. I grew up in a very middle-class family in Oklahoma City. My great-grandparents started some of the first grocery stores in the state. And the next generation divided itself between restaurants and grocery stores, but mostly restaurants. They were typical American places: diners and steakhouses. During the drive-in restaurant craze, back in the late fifties and early sixties, my family was really big in all of that, too.

My father married into that family and he didn't want to do any of those things and he decided that the future was in barbeque. Even though my father wasn't a cook at all, he was a very perceptive guy and he was really creative and he decided he was just going to learn how to be a great pit master and he really devoted his time to doing that. So I grew up in a barbeque restaurant. Oklahoma barbeque is sort of like a cross between Texas and Kansas styles. Where I grew up it was eaten in a full-fledged family restaurant. In fact, one of the nicest restaurants in our town was a barbeque restaurant.

My playground growing up was the back kitchen. Even before I was old enough to help, I used to be able to go into the walk-in and I'd get stuff and play with it. From an early age I had the sense that I could express myself through food. You have to get your own voice in your cooking. That's what I learned with the very good cooks even back then; they each had their own voices. And I learned that in a barbeque restaurant. We did it differently from other people but we were all working within the same region. We felt we were the guardians of a local tradition, so maybe I was instilled with the idea of regional cooking then.

I didn't realize till I hit puberty that everything in my house smelled of hickory smoke, because that's what we used to cook over. And then once you start thinking about girls when you hit puberty, you suddenly realize that everything you own smells like smoke and the girls would get close to you and go, "What's that smell?" That embarrassed me. All the clothes that I ever wore working at the restaurant were segregated from the rest of my clothes.

I was at a very impressionable age, fourteen, when I first went to Mexico. In some ways it was the dream vacation. I planned this first family vacation on an airplane, and my folks were sort of against it, but I was so passionate about taking this trip that they agreed to go.

So I was predisposed to love it. I just didn't know how much I would love it once I got there. In some ways I felt more at home there than in the place where I had grown up. There was something about arriving in Mexico City at ten o'clock at night with the streets thronging with people. We stayed in this fabulous old hotel, Hotel del Prado, that's been gone since the 1985 earthquake, but it was right on the Alameda Park. When I got to the room and threw open the blinds, I looked down on this scene in the park at about eleven o'clock at night. There are all these street vendors and live musicians, a culture that was teeming with life, not at all what I grew up with. It was what I'd always hoped I would someday find, and there I was at fourteen finding it.

I didn't really focus on the food on that first trip as I did the culture. And the culture is what led me in college to study Spanish-language literature and Latin American studies. So I kept going back and forth to Mexico doing different projects. Then I went to graduate school studying the relationship between language and culture. I made my way through school cooking, mostly catering. Then when I got toward the end of my Ph.D. program I realized I had forgotten what was really my true passion, the relationship between food and culture. I decided to switch gears and went back to studying food and culture and the relationship between the two, but that wasn't satisfying to me. I knew I had to actually cook the stuff.

That's when I decided to really focus on Mexico and decided to write a cookbook of regional Mexican specialties. I saved up all this money, enough to live for a year, while I wrote the book. About three months into it, I realized that this was in fact a lifetime project and that I was going to have to figure out a way to support myself.

I had been contacted by a small chain of Mexican American restaurants in Los Angeles to do some consulting work for them. This was back in the early eighties when Mexican food in the United States was going from just the simple combination plate to something a little more varied, so restaurant owners were in need of someone who could help them advance their menus. I started working with the idea that I could work with them for three months and then be off for three months. My wife, Deann, and I did that for years. Each time that we had a three-month chunk we'd put ourselves into a different region, immersing ourselves in its culture.

I had done a lot of research, and had some firsthand experience, so

I would know where to go and set up shop, and I would sort of radiate out from that. Over the next five years we did that very systematically. I'd come from a Ph.D. program where we had to do anthropological field research, so I just set it up to be a project like that. You go in and see what people are doing. You don't go in there knowing the answers, but with a completely open mind to see what people say and do.

And that's one of the reasons that my work has always been so different than others', because many come at it from a prescriptive standpoint where they're saying, this is the way it should be done, this is the best way and everyone should follow me. I was saying, what are people really cooking? What do they say about it? What are the stories that they tell about it? What role does this dish play in their culture? Is it something you eat on a Wednesday night? Is it something you eat once a year? Is it seasonal? And if it's seasonal, how does it relate to other things that happen during that season? Does it fit into the liturgical calendar? Where does it fit in the whole culture? I wasn't trying to show people how it should be.

I also was not interested in the specialties that home cooks had come up with as their family recipe. This has made my work very different than other people's, too. Some people will go into a culture and say, "I found the person who makes the very best X, and I'm going to share their recipe with you." Instead, I ate the dish made by several different people. Regional cooks all think they're doing it the right way. Then I would write a recipe that everybody would consider to be a good recipe, not just one family.

So *Authentic Mexican* came out in 1987, and I realized that there was so little knowledge of the regional specialties of Mexico in the U.S. and I could keep writing about it, but that wasn't going to be as dramatic and influential as if I opened a restaurant. There was nowhere you could go to learn the kinds of things that I had learned doing my research in Mexico, so I thought I just have to kind of forge the thing myself. I just have to open a restaurant and figure out how to make this food in a restaurant setting. Since I'd grown up in the restaurant world and I'd done massive amounts of catering, I had a sense of how you would scale things up, whether it was a meal for six people or a meal for two hundred people. So I just plunged in and opened Frontera Grill, and for nearly the next ten years I did nothing but just work on the development of transforming those traditional Mexican recipes into a restaurant sort of format. I worked a position on our line for five years. There was nowhere in the U.S. where I could learn our food, so I had to be on the line. You have to do the work.

I really gave my whole soul to that whole process because I wanted to establish my approach to Mexican cooking. Translation is what I do, and it is inspired by what I did in linguistics. A word-for-word translation means nothing. It won't have the power. You really have to get into it. I am not looking for a literal translation in food. If I tried to speak Oaxacan in Chicago it wouldn't work. The corn is different; the epazote is different. The very culture of food is different. In the U.S., 95 percent of tortillas are flour, in Mexico 95 percent are corn. That's just one problem of bringing this cuisine to the United States: people have no idea how to relate to those corn tortillas. At an average sitting, someone in Mexico would eat six to ten tortillas along with their main course. To get someone to eat one tortilla with their main course in the U.S. is a huge feat. They don't want to fill up with tortillas. They think it's just like eating a whole bunch of bread. But it's actually a part of the flavor and balance of the meal.

So we try to figure out how to achieve the authenticity of flavor—which is what I'm going for in my food—and still feel it's the right balance. Most people will go along with us, and we encourage them to eat the tortillas because we make absolutely superb tortillas, which have never been reheated, so they're hot off the griddle. They tend to be seductive, and people will eat one of those and then two and . . .

We have a whole department of people that do the masa work. They press out using the two-plated press. The hand patting of the tortillas is sort of a thing of the past. Most people don't even know how to do it, but most people know how to press it out between the two iron plates. Then they're just baked on a regular griddle. The whole idea is that it looks incredibly simple and it's just this cooked corn that gets ground up and there's a little water added to it and that's it. But with every simple task it's really hard to do it right. That's why we have a whole team of people that do nothing but work with masa stuff. It's really hard to learn it if you didn't learn it from the time you were a little kid. It's one of those touches that you just have to get when you're little. I can do it okay but, man, I can't do it anywhere near what the people in that group in our restaurant do.

For me, Mexican food is built on bold flavor, especially in central and southern Mexico, which is what I focus on. But it's also a very complex cuisine, with a finely tuned balance. There's always a fresh element that contrasts to a well-cooked element, and there's always brightness in the salsas. It's like the tongue is always firing on all cylinders because you get some bitterness, some sweetness, some acid, and some saltiness. It's the same kind of thing as barbeque sauce, where you get all those elements balancing, but barbeque tends to balance more toward sweet than Mexican does. Mexican food doesn't typically trend toward sweet; in fact, most salsas will have very few sweet elements in them except super-ripe tomatoes. So when you eat Mexican food in the United States, where it's typically made with underripe tomatoes, it goes way acid, and in Mexico you get more of a balance of the sweet because you get riper tomatoes.

Still, there are limits that I have always placed on myself in terms of the authenticity. The truth of the matter is our restaurants are nice restaurants, and in nice restaurants in Mexico you wouldn't, for example, find *tacos de cabeza,* tacos made from stewed head meat. You go to a place where that's really their specialty, and everyone goes there for that. It might be a street stall, it might be a taquería, but that's what their specialty is. I do more elaborate cuisine. So I've chosen not to get involved in that form of authenticity. Partly because it's harder to convince Americans that *tacos de cabeza* are going to be the fabulous thing that they are. You have so many hurdles to jump across. You put a black mole from Oaxaca in front of them, and they're suddenly just enthralled with the thing. Because it's unlike anything they've tasted, created out of flavors that just hang out there in the world, but they don't know anything about them.

But I also don't serve such tacos, or grasshoppers, for that matter, because it turns a culture into strangers. People eat all parts of all animals everywhere in the world pretty much except in the United States, where we've become so narrow about all this stuff. I think that shows us to perhaps be lacking in our culture. People often ask me, "What's the weirdest thing you've ever eaten in Mexico? I heard that they eat armadillos." It's saying, "They're weird down there." It makes it into the "other." And I want us to be together in this whole thing.

Our restaurant is twenty years old now, and as our restaurant developed, people came along that needed to be taking leadership roles. I started writing more and doing TV work, so now I kind of balance my time between all of them. What I have always hoped is that when customers have eaten a meal at our restaurants they have gone through an experience, and we have been able to bring them something that might be new to them and memorable. Mexico has one of the most generous spirits. In Mexican Spanish there's a term, *sobremesa*, for when the meal is finished and you're just sitting enjoying the company of the people you ate with. I hope we've been able to instill some of that philosophy, too. The most valuable lesson of Mexican food might well occur when the eating is done.

David Bouley

Chef David Bouley has been a presence in the New York food scene for more than two decades. He learned his craft from acclaimed chefs, including Roger Vergé, Paul Bocuse, Joel Robuchon, Gaston Lenôtre, and Frédy Girardet, in restaurants such as Le Cirque, Le Périgord, and La Côte Basque. David opened Bouley and followed it with Bouley Bakery, which he later expanded to include a market and a café. His widely acclaimed first cookbook, *East of Paris*, is filled with reinterpreted Eastern European recipes as experienced in his Austro-Hungarian restaurant, Danube. He has received the James Beard Foundation Award for Best Chef, and his restaurant Bouley has been honored with the James Beard Award for Best Restaurant.

My first teacher was my grandmother. My grandparents were already in their late thirties when they moved here from France. They weren't going to change their lives. They came here because my grandfather had broken his back on a submarine in San Francisco in the French navy, and then when he came back into service, the Americans put him into the American navy, and when he got out of that, they gave him a passport. He was an engineer, and his family had three pas-

43

try shops in Nancy and Metz, so he grew up in pastry shops. He made baguettes. I can still see the towel on the old ceramic white little oven rolled over with baguettes rising there, and he made brioche three or four times a week. In fact, my mother made homemade bread until I was fifteen years old. We never had bread brought in from outside.

They bought a farm up in Woonsocket and land in Jamestown, Rhode Island, on the beach. I spent a lot of time with them there. That's where my grandmother started teaching me how to cook. The earliest time I can remember with her, I may have been five or six, and she had the oven door open, and she was on her knees basting a rabbit with prunes, one of our favorite dishes. And I was standing next to her watching her, and she gave me the spoon, and I tried it, and I threw a little butter and I made a fire, because I threw it all over the side of the oven. The oven was just barely lower than my eyes. And I was excited about the fire, what was going on, and the smell, but I was probably more excited about watching her do what she did. So how is a chef's passion ignited? Well, it demands being around a special person: someone that knows great product, someone that has been taught technique, and someone who is very generous with their love and their emotion. And those three, when they hit you, there's no escape.

I went and looked at The French Culinary School, when it was in New Britain, Connecticut, and I was out of there in two hours. I never saw so many tattoos and guys smoking. It was mostly military people that were going into this to get a job. And I didn't feel any passion, which I'd felt at my grandmother's house, or even understanding of product. It was more like a trade. So then I went to school and I studied business administration, and I thought I could do something like that, but then I realized I need emotion in my work, whatever I do. I want to make people feel something. If I choose to work this hard, I want to make sure they can feel it. I want to have an effect on someone like my grandmother did during those seven-hour Sunday meals when she placed the platter on the table and said, *"Voilà!"*

I moved around a bit. In 1975, I went to work in New Mexico. I managed the Pink Adobe Restaurant in Santa Fe, which still exists today. Then I went to Aspen, and I skied for a while, and I realized I could cook soup, because all the ski team people wanted me to give them the recipes. I ran a soup kitchen with a bunch of people in San Francisco, and gradually I started thinking, well, okay, you know, I need to cook, so let's go to France. But still I was hesitant. I didn't go to France to cook. I went to France to study art, because I still wasn't convinced that cooking could ever match the emotional power it had early in my life. So I could continue living in Paris, I got a job at a bistro called Henri Bostel. The owner had a little food column for thirty years in the *Pariscope* weekly. All the chefs would go there—Bocuse, Vergé, Guérard—and that's how I started to go work for them.

It was then that I started the process that is so important—and that going to Europe can really amplify—of figuring out what you are about. Again, I was lucky to have great teachers. You can say that teaching is passing on information but you have to put it in terms that click for the person. For example, when I first started baking, I was at the Moulin de Mougins and I was working crazy hours, and Mr. Vergé thought I was insane when I asked him if I could work with his baker. Because that meant I had to be there at four a.m. and I didn't finish until midnight. So I started with this eighty-year-old baker. The first day he put a hand in the flour and a hand in the air and said, "Baking is now matching these two together with the temperature of

45

the water." Suddenly baking struck me as something I could someday understand. The next day we made rolls. He'd finished five trays before I'd done one.

At Girardet's I learned another lesson. One day Mr. Girardet came over to me when I was taking the skin off tomatoes and he said to me, "You're not talking to the tomatoes." He put his hand on a tomato and he left, and he never talked to me for the whole day. I said to Gray Kunz, who was there also, "What's he talking about?" Eventually I came to understand what it was, through cooking. Every ingredient is different—every tomato, every bit of fish. There are so many different variables—the fish could be out of the same filet, but different parts of the fish might have more fat, or the pans are different, the heat is different. So all these things you have to pay so much attention to, and I call that a conversation.

If you're having a conversation with what you're doing, it's important. One time, Bocuse came to the kitchen and on the way out he told the staff, he said, "Some of you cook too comfortable. I don't see fear in your face when you're cooking." And I don't think he meant that you should look like you're going to have a nervous breakdown, but I think that some of them were probably just cooking like, "Oh, I just cooked my twentieth piece of halibut tonight, and I'm cooking it the same as I did the first one." Well, that doesn't work. And he knew that, and I knew that, so that's his way, and that was my way to get someone to actually pay attention to that kind of focus, to be that close, because you will find a lot of different things if you get that close.

I'd opened Sutter 500, in San Francisco, with Hubert Keller, but then I went back to France and I moved around some more. I came back with lots of ideas of lighter food and I put them into place at Montrachet. Cutting out cream meant restructuring a kitchen. In many French restaurants at that time there'd be four or five cooks doing two hundred, two hundred and fifty covers. One of the reasons they were able to do that is because cream stabilized a lot of their recipes. Once it had come to a boil, a cream sauce could sit forever. So cutting that one ingredient out meant figuring out a new way to approach the demands of a service. Doing French cooking without cream at a professional level took a little thinking.

When I opened Bouley, I knew I was going to be in the kitchen for ten years—that's how long the lease was, and I knew it was going to be almost like a prison for me, because that's what it's going to take. So I put up beautiful paintings of places I knew and loved in the south of France. I figured I'd go out and sit in the dining room in my ten-minute break in the afternoon and look at those paintings and feel like I'm on vacation. Well, I did go out and do that, but it wasn't quite a prison. Wall Street was much more active than today. Goldman Sachs would do a million and a half dollars in sales with us a year, and many people came four or five times a week, and they didn't look at the menu. "Tell him to cook—I want four fish, I want two meats." "Today I've got plenty of time. I want six fish, three or four meats, I want cheese." "Today I'm out of time. I want two fish and no meat."

That suited me fine. I work best when someone pushes me to the corner and throws food at me and says, "Cook." I wait until the last minute, and then I do it. If I think too far in advance, I'll mess it up. I have to be spontaneous. So I was the right person for these people who would come in constantly. Customers told me years later they hadn't seen the menu in five years. So you have, let's say, forty people like that in one night, at seven or eight tables. Well, they'd already been in three nights that week. You don't want a captain to come to you and say, "You know, on the way out, he said Tuesday's was much better than tonight." So you would say, "This is horrible. We messed up." You know, you'd be really upset about that. So you'd have to keep the ball in the air.

Everything you do in cooking adds to internal confidence. At Montrachet, I had lightened French cooking. When I started thinking about the cooking of the Austro-Hungarian empire, the ingredients were different but the process was the same. I first was drawn to it through the art of the Secessionist period, between 1890 and 1920, when all the artists and intellectuals were living in Vienna. So I wanted to know, what is the Secessionist period? It's profound. It's sort of like New York City. In terms of food it was a challenge just to get people to understand it's not just Wiener schnitzel and bratwurst. If the monarchy had continued, it probably would be one of the most refined cuisines on the planet. In terms of ingredients, it was fantastic. They had Venice for a fish market. And I think what intrigued me about the cuisine was that it was slow-cooked. There was a lot of soul in this food, and you have great ingredients. Pumpkinseed, elderflower, paprika that is so fresh that it looks like lipstick when you touch it and when they sell it in stores it has an expiration date on it. The paprika has to be used within so many weeks. At that time in America it was sitting in a warehouse in Oklahoma for fourteen years, and then we get a little can of it and it's like granulated sand. So the variables were so unique to me. I thought I knew about paprika, and there I was learning about paprika.

When I first moved to New York, I didn't think people really knew

what fresh fish was here. That's a huge statement, and I'm going to get some flack for that, but, really, the processing and everything was so different than catching and eating a fish that was just pulled out of the ocean. Sure, you could find great fish, but a fish that is line-pulled out of the sea is completely different. Growing up in Jamestown, I swam in those waters. In the late sixties, we used to go and work part-time there, all the way from Old Seabrook all the way up to the Cape. We'd have part-time summer jobs working around fish, fish restaurants, and earn part-time money with day boats. I knew what a day boat was. They're only four or five hours out at sea so they can get back before the tide. They leave at three thirty or four and get back by twelve thirty. That's not fish from a trawler that's out for a week at a time.

So I thought people should know what a day boat was, and I started writing, "Chatham day boat fish," on my menu at Bouley. And they used to make fun of me then. Gael Greene used to make fun—she'd pick things up at the end of the meal and ask the waiter, "Now, where is this pear from?" Today I see Chatham and other place names all over menus and I think it's great. It's nice, for example, to see a cheese from Colchester, Connecticut. That's about nine miles from where I grew up, and I thought the only thing they knew in that town was drag racing. But for young people I think it's important to understand where recipes come from. I realized this at Girardet, when I saw the collection of antique cookbooks Mr. Girardet kept upstairs. At the time he was the most prolific cook in the world. He was on *60 Minutes*; he had two full pages in the *Times*. He was not a professionally trained chef who spent all his minutes reading antique cooking books. So I think at the time you're learning lots of things, it's important for you to understand where ingredients come from. You will build on that. You can learn a recipe very quickly, but understanding the product and the philosophy around it will give you more recipes.

It turns out I didn't know as much about fish as I thought I did. It wasn't until I started to learn about Japanese food that I understood that. I have a friend in New York and his name is Yoshiki Tsuji and he owns a cooking school in Osaka and Tokyo. Some years ago I was on the way to Thailand to cook for the royal family, and he told me, "Stop in Tokyo, spend a week with us." And we had the time, so we stopped. For me it was a realization about food. The Japanese approach to food is so different than the Western world. Fish, for example, is delivered swimming in big plastic bags with water. The way they would say it is, "We don't treat our fish any other way than the way you treat your animals. You wouldn't fill boxes with animals and let them suffocate then put them on a truck and cut open their stomachs three days later. Why do you do that with your fish?"

Most of the fish you eat in a sushi bar, until you go to Japan, you think is raw. But there are only a few things that are actually raw fish, which might be an oyster, possibly a scallop, maybe a shrimp and tuna. Everything has been seasoned with salt for a few minutes to detox the fish and to cleanse the fish, and then the salt is rinsed off in a salt-and-vinegar-water bath.

So that was my second day. The first day was dashi, which is their stock of all their sauces. We made twenty-five kinds of dashi. But when I realized I didn't know anything about the preparation of fish in a sushi bar, I wanted to. I was very attracted to learn more, and as they explained to me, when you eat a raw fish that's fresh out of the ocean it's very mealy, the fish; when it's very fresh it's not a pleasant taste or texture, and the salt cleanses the fish of any impurities but also gives the fish a texture, a crunch that we like. We think that's the way it is, when it's raw—but it's not that way when it's raw. And I learned how to kill the fish—at the spinal cord, so the fish relaxes like a balloon losing air, and there are no impurities and the flesh is very clear, almost transparent.

So this, on my second day, made me realize that I could apply a lot of this to my French cooking. I've always loved Japanese food. It's light, it's clean, gives me a lot of energy. It was great to eat after service at two o'clock in the morning, when you're working in the restaurant business.

But through the Japanese and through the Tsuji school, I've learned that there is so much more that we can apply to our Western world of training. Their obsession with the highest level of the raw product fascinates me. There's a chef in Tokyo, at Mibu, and he went to cook with El Bulli, in Spain. He brought five hundred kilos of water with him from the mountains in Japan to Barcelona. He took five trailer trucks to do one table of eight three nights in a row. So I went to eat at this restaurant in Tokyo, with Mr. Tsuji. There are only two tables with four people in this restaurant. And Mr. Tsuji said, "He's going to come out, he's going to bow, and he's going to say, 'I try my best,' and he's going to leave." So when he came out, I told Mr. Tsuji, "Tell him that's the closest that I've ever been to the highest and most intimate level of nature." And he told him that, and he grabbed my hand and he sat down, and three hours later we were still talking about grapefruit and water and oranges and things like these.

When I worked at Bocuse, he once invited me out to lunch, which he used to do with particular people. He always stayed in touch with his staff; he was curious about what they were thinking. And one of the questions he asked me was what did I think a chef was. Before I could answer, he told me that a chef was someone who could do everything in the kitchen in every department better and faster than anyone else. Just by asking me the question, he was exemplifying the answer. A chef has to have strength in leadership, lead by example, and understand they are teaching. If you don't have those three skills it doesn't really matter how well you can cook. A chef has to be a leader, has to be a person who trains staff, has to be someone whom people are going to respect. Your kitchen basically votes to work for you. So it's like they nominated you to become their leader in their profession. So you have to be responsible for them. Number one, you teach them not to make concessions with products. Number two, you teach them to maintain strength with technique. And number three, you teach them generosity of spirit, what I learned from my grandmother, to put in the extra love.

That takes discipline, because sometimes you're tired, sometimes you're in a rush, sometimes you just think they won't notice the difference. But people will feel the emotion in your cooking if that number three discipline is there, and when you don't do that, they'll have a nice meal but they won't find that emotion in the food. A chef has to take on these responsibilities. It can seem overwhelming. Sometimes I want to say, I am a cook. As the Japanese chef said, I try my best.

Chef's Story **David Bouley**

Daniel Boulud

Daniel Boulud was raised near Lyon, France. In 1993 he opened his much-heralded restaurant Daniel, which was awarded four stars by the *New York Times* and praised as one of the best in the world. He has since opened DB Bistro Moderne and Café Boulud in New York, a Café Boulud in Palm Beach, and Daniel Boulud Brasserie in Las Vegas. He has received countless culinary honors, including Chef of the Year awards from *Bon Appétit* and the James Beard Foundation, which also named him the country's Outstanding Restaurateur in 2006. His most recent cookbook is *Braise*.

In the old days in France you could have two kinds of vans. One was a Citroën that had kind of corrugated iron sides. People called it *le tube*. The other was the Renault Estafette. The engines were about the same, both weak, but the Renault was considered to be better. It had heat. On Saturday mornings my father and I would load the Estafette and head down to the market in Lyon while it was still dark. We had a farm about twenty miles outside the city. Because it was hilly country, we had to grow a little bit of everything and we also made cheese. We grew onions, zucchini, garlic, potatoes, essentially everything you could need for cooking—except for microgreens. How did we ever manage without them?

We also had wonderful customers who came to the farm, often wealthy, influential people from Lyon. We had the biggest surgeon from Lyon. We had a countess from Italy, the Countess di Volti, who was living in the neighborhood. I told her I wanted to become a chef and was going to a nearby culinary school. I thought I would become a chef for a cafeteria. But after two months at the school, I told my mother I couldn't. I said, "No, I hate this school. It's no good. The food they're doing is no good." I could tell there was no connection between what I knew from home and what I was learning in school. As much as you need to learn the classics, I think they've got to taste good.

Well, when the countess found out, she said, "I'm going to find you the best restaurant there is." She went around to the three-star and two-star places where she used to eat and asked them if they could take me. It could take up to a two years' wait to get an apprentice opening in some places, and she was trying to shorten the process for me. Finally she nailed down Nandron, which was one of the best restaurants in Lyon, a two-star restaurant where I could start in two months' time.

What was interesting about Nandron was that it was a real traditional Lyonnaise restaurant with a full brigade. They used to call me the Beaver because I was quite short. Not that I've grown that much since. The name was also due to my being forced to spend a lot of time in the wettest part of the kitchen. When you were just starting out as an apprentice, you were just pushed into the sink, and you had to clean everyone's salads, so they called me the Beaver because I was always flailing under mountains of greens.

One of my favorite jobs was going to the market in Lyon, where the chef went to get what we needed. It was two blocks away from the restaurant, and I would carry the cases back. There was a tiny street on the side of *les halles* [covered markets] where they were cleaning all the meat guts and making casings and washing them with hot water in the street, so there were always clouds of steam. I loved all the fantastic smells of the market, the charcuterie, the *fromagerie,* the fish, the meat, the game, the mushrooms. All the great chefs were there: Bocuse, Alain Chapel. To us they were already the giants of the *cuisine.* They were ruling the place, basically, and they criss-crossed the halls. I was following my boss.

Because we were just a block away we didn't need to have things delivered, and we didn't need to put our purchases in a car. All the other chefs, even Bocuse, all of them had to put everything in their cars. I just had to carry ours to the restaurant, so I was making at least five trips every morning. Afterward all the chefs met in the café. I can still see them in their leather jackets in the winter. They'd have *tablier de sapeur,* breaded tripe steak, always oysters in the winter, and a good wine, and of course cheese and pâté and charcuterie and all the stuff you need to really get started in the morning.

When I look back I realize I was learning something very important at Nandron, and that was delicacy. At home we would just cook the crayfish and serve them. At Nandron I learned how to prepare them and peel them perfectly. At Nandron you wouldn't even know a chicken had bones. At my home we just split it in eight pieces with all the bones and the neck and the head and the gizzard and the liver and we just cooked everything together and it tasted delicious. I think in a restaurant you are transforming food into something wonderful, but sometimes by trying to make it perfect and elegant you kind of lose a bit of the rusticity of flavor and simplicity as well. I think my food is constantly going back and forth between rusticity and elegance. I find that makes for very soulful food. I love food with soul. I need it.

You kind of know when your apprenticeship is over. You know every station in the kitchen and you know as much as the *chefs de partie*. In fact, it's often the apprentice who's telling them how the chef wants things done. I spent three and a half years at Nandron. Monsieur Nandron liked me, but the chef didn't. My apprenticeship ended with the chef chasing me around the kitchen with a ladle.

I went to Georges Blanc in 1973. He is in the Bresse region, in a town called Vonnas, about a hundred miles north of Lyon. My parents brought me there and we arrived on a Sunday afternoon after the big lunch service. There were girls everywhere. I'd never worked in a restaurant where there was a girl. Here there were waitresses and cocktail waitresses—and they were looking at me, checking out the new cook. I thought, "Wow, this is a nice place."

It was the first time I was working in a country inn. Weekends were crazy because we were doing about a hundred and fifty, but weekdays we'd do about sixty. Georges Blanc's grandmother had started the restaurant, and it was an amazing estate in the middle of the village. At the time it was still a very local restaurant. It was wonderful to see the blend of very sophisticated customers and local people. Every Thursday we had the village market, and all the locals would come to the bar of the restaurant and eat lunch.

The food at Blanc was very authentic, very regional. He had the crayfish from les Dombes and Bresse chickens and escargot and, in winter, lots of game. He had a wonderful team of very ambitious young chefs. But it wasn't the structure of Nandron, which had so many layers between everybody. To be there at seventeen was wonderful. I was already at a level above many of the cooks my age, who might have only worked in some other local restaurant. So I felt very responsible, I could share my knowledge and was very confident about my work and my skill. But I understood I had to keep learning.

Every time I wanted to work for another chef I would talk to my current chef first. I would say, "I've done my time and I want to move on. I would like to go here, here or here." You have to have a few options, because he can't just pick up the phone and say, "Do you have a job for my young chef?" Also the cooks were much more stable than now, so to nail down a job you had to be patient. Today, the turnover is frantic.

Eventually I would go from Blanc to Roger Vergé and Michel Guérard. Looking back, I see how every restaurant went into shaping me. Nandron gave me the authenticity of classic cuisine; Blanc, the authenticity of regional cooking; Michel Guérard was the most intellectual chef I've worked for. I discovered Daniel through a little bit of each of them. But I feel I really understood Vergé, not only as a person but culinarily as well. He was a chef who had developed a cuisine on his own, and I think he touched me a lot by this. There was a blend of sun and Provence; his best dishes were adapted from Provençal cooking and made sophisticated by Roger Vergé, so they were very complex but with very good technique as well.

Ever since I was fifteen I'd understood that one of the most wonderful things about cooking is that it opens the world to you. Monsieur Nandron was very diversified, and he used to cater banquets at the prefecture, the town hall. I helped prepare meals for the president of France and presidents of African countries. Because I was with the cooking staff, I'd be given a *laissez-passer*, what would here be called an "all-areas access pass." So here was this big building with lots of police around it, and I could just

stroll in. I was very impressed by that. Coming to America was a bit of the same thing; it just wouldn't have happened if I wasn't a cook. I also think I wouldn't be the same chef if I'd stayed in France. Being a French chef in New York, I try to remain true to French cuisine. That doesn't mean that I can't evolve, but I am very conscious that I represent something. It's not a hindrance; I feel it gives me enormous liberty. I can use ingredients from anywhere, but at the same time there are still always roots, technique, and the tastes that certain techniques impart, all those things that give support to a dish.

I first came over to be private chef at the French embassy in Washington. In the first week I went to see Jean-Louis Palladin, who was chef at Jean-Louis at the Watergate. I knew him because when he'd had a restaurant in France it wasn't far from Guérard's, and when we closed for the season we'd have our closing party at his restaurant. There has never been someone like Jean-Louis, and through him, by the end of my second week, I knew every chef in Washington.

I think in life, besides having talent, you need a little bit of luck. For me each job has presented a challenge and an opportunity. From Washington, I came to be co-chef at the Polo Lounge at the Westbury Hotel in New York. Actually, I was more like a sous-chef who worried about everything. Then I took over the Regence at the Plaza Athénée. It's hard to come here when you are young and you want to prove you can do it. When you arrive in the U.S. as a chef who has proven who he is, you really have ammunition. You can say, "If I don't like it, I'll go somewhere else." But if you are very young and they give you a stage, your first stage, you want to prove to them that you can do it. So for that, you work until you can prove it.

At the Plaza Athénée, in New York, I had total freedom to do what I wanted to do. The only thing I didn't like was the politics of the hotel, which I hated. I could see I was not made for such a structure, where there were too many people making decisions who didn't have a clue about running a restaurant. When I went around the corner to Le Cirque, it was very different. Sirio started in the business very young. He had a true passion for the business and he had complete confidence in what he was doing in the front of the house. He said, "Give me thirty percent creativity. The rest has to be food I'm comfortable offering my customers." For me that was as it should be. It was his business. I wasn't there to destroy his business; I was there to enhance it.

I think it's very dangerous for a chef to try and put too much of their imprint on a business that already exists. It's sometimes very difficult. It's always a very, very slow process. But I think Sirio knew I was okay. Paul Bocuse had told him so, and he'd known me since I was fourteen, following him around the market of Lyon.

Young cooks have to have the passion and the understanding. But they also have to understand their place. When I was an apprentice I didn't have the right to give my opinion on anything. When you work for a chef, you cannot change anything from what the chef wants, and it's only by perfecting what the chef asks you to do that you become a better cook. I think we chefs are emotional about everything that's happening in our kitchens. When you lose a cook, it is hard; and when you train a new one, you are committing to providing them with a lot of support. When they get to be the chef de cuisine in my restaurants, that's when I need them to be creative, within the possibilities of the price point we have created and we need to respect. I give them total freedom, but the goal is to practice my philosophy of cooking. Ironically, it is more of a Daniel Boulud restaurant that way than if I fax them the menu and say this is what you're cooking today.

My greatest challenge is to try and spend more time in the kitchen. I spend about five hours a day, which is not enough because I spend them mostly during the service and that is not when you dream. In the afternoon, when you do the *mise en place* [prep work], that's when you communicate and create. I would like to participate as much in the preparation as the finishing. And that is part of cooking; the preparation is half the pleasure.

I won't say I have "come back" to braising, because there's always been braising in my cooking. For me it represents that cooking style when a house is filled with beautiful smells. Braising has lots of soul, and playing with it allows me to play with traditions. All countries have their own way of adapting certain cuts of meat. Lamb, for example, is quite universal. From India to Morocco to France to Italy, there are many ways of accommodating that ingredient. I have tried to extract some inspiration from that. I'm not pretending that my Indian cooking is totally Indian, but it has certain strong flavors. Is my French cooking totally French? Not always. I'm less and less interested in labels.

The France I grew up in is a memory. In terms of cooking, there was the *nationale sept*, a two-lane road that was a highway that went south from Paris, and many of the greatest restaurants of the past century were right there on the *nationale sept*. People were much more faithful to restaurants. Every year they would go and visit the same ones, and it was part of their life. It was part of their relationship with the restaurant, and I think they became part of the soul of those places. Today the people of Vonnas may be able to go to Hawaii but they're not going to Thursday lunch at Georges Blanc. And so that changes a lot. What happens is that something is destroyed, a little bit of that wonderful fiber France was built on.

So I can feel nostalgic, but I also feel hopeful. Evolution is a necessity in cooking. Chefs today have to figure out how to offer a version of their cooking at a lower price. That's a challenge. In France there are a lot of young people today who understand tradition is something you have to protect. Perhaps braising is my way of continuing a tradition. Every chef I ever worked for braised. During the game season we would braise, and in spring, too; there were seasonal ways of applying braising. I've always carried a little bit of that with me. There is often the idea of braising in my dishes even though it may not be visually obvious.

For example, we make a ravioli of beef cheeks with a little bit of ginger. We mix in a little mascarpone and we put braising *jus* inside. So it has a very traditional flavor of beef braised in red wine, but the carrots bring out a little sweetness that juxtaposes very well. That's how I like to play with braising; I keep the traditional meaning, the traditional idea, but I'll definitely flip the textures and the combinations in a way that isn't remotely what the classic was. A dish like that sends me back, through all the restaurants I worked at. It can send me to the civet we used to make at Nandron. And it can send me even further back, to the dark mornings when it was just my father and I in the loaded-down Renault van heading to the market in Lyon. We may not have gone very fast, but we were always warm.

Anthony Bourdain

New York City native Anthony Bourdain is executive chef at Brasseries les Halles, with two bistros in New York City and others in Washington, D.C., and Miami. His memoir *Kitchen Confidential* was a bestseller, and his Food Network series resulted in his book *A Cook's Tour.*

My roommates got me into cooking. It was during summer vacation and they were sick of me freeloading, and they said, "We got you a dishwasher job. Now you can pay rent." This was in Provincetown, out at Cape Cod, and I looked around and I saw the cooks, and I thought, wow, there's no lying in here, you know. These guys are good at something. You're able to, at the end of the day, say, "Hey, I kept up my end. I did something with my hands." Immediate gratification, coupled with the party atmosphere, brought me in, and over time I found myself getting more and more serious about it, and I reached a point where I just wanted to be good at it.

Back then, in the early seventies, you were guaranteeing yourself heartbreak to try to cook well, to do things right, because more often than not it wouldn't be appreciated. So the people I met who started to take a perverse, elitist pride in knowing what good food was and

how it should be or could be prepared better were also cooking effi-
ciently and at reasonably high quality. I was very impressed with
that. I recognized the pride they had and the fact that cooking was
a subculture and a misunderstood and underappreciated one, so, of
course, I dug that.

There's no question that as the status of chefs and cooks has risen—
however annoying the celebrity chef phenomenon is—it has created
real hope and expectations for cooks. You have a real possibility of
some status and prestige, some financial success and security. Those
are important to building the kind of unit pride in kitchens. I haven't
seen anyone spit in the soup for twenty-five years. That would be
unthinkable in any kind of self-respecting restaurant or kitchen now,
because the people you work with would consider that treason.

When I went to The Culinary Institute of America, it was the
first time I understood the discipline professional cooking demands.
There's just straight-up discipline for yourself but also the discipline
of the team. It's not really esprit de corps. One person is in charge. You
can't have a hippie commune in the kitchen, where everyone is giving
their input. At the end of the day you must produce. Eight different
plates have to go out to the right tables in proper order, sequence, and
condition. And to disseminate that kind of information, to delegate
those kinds of instructions in an orderly fashion, I think, is always
going to take an autocratic society.

So there's a certain militaristic aspect to it, but at the same time
this is a mentoring business. One cook teaches another—often under
brutal pressure. It's "Okay, I'm going to show you everything I know
that it has taken me twenty-five, thirty years to learn painfully. I'm
working in a very busy restaurant. I'm about to invest a lot of time

that I don't have in showing you everything I know. I'd like to know now, not later, if you're going to go home crying on our first busy Saturday night."

When you first arrive in a restaurant, having gone to culinary school is not that much of an advantage. It's an advantage in the sense that the chef can look over and say, "Give me a *brunoise,*" and he doesn't have to demonstrate, but not much more than that. You're still learning. The chefs might take you under their wing, but more often than not it's the Latino guy who maybe started out as a dishwasher or a salad man or a prep cook. These are the people who are doing the actual cooking, holding the place up. And believe me, they know the drill. They know that the more privileged kids who come out of cooking school pass through a kitchen for a year or a six-month apprenticeship and then they're gone. And even though these guys like to kick ass, and taking time to show someone how it's done slows them down, they do it because that's what cooks do. So in the best conditions, a young cook has everyone from the chef to other cooks putting pressure on them. I think there has to be that pressure. I'm not talking about throwing food or putting hands on people or personally insulting them, but a chef has to find out who's going to make it, who isn't, and who's worth investing time in.

I flamed out initially as a chef. I screwed up and then I spent a lot of time bouncing around. I enjoyed not having to fire people. I'd really had my fill of that, but I found myself a cook who was a de facto chef. I was running the kitchen to protect myself and the people that I cared about. I came out of knucklehead kitchens with a bunch of guys sitting around getting high and drinking, and we were all in it because it was fun. Often I was the only one who really spoke En-

glish, not that English is the language of kitchens; it's always a kind of weird mix. Some of the best cooks in fact can only talk trash.

I think what attracts us all is that a kitchen is one of the last meritocracies of all workplaces. You are rewarded for your skill. There's no lying in the kitchen. You can talk all you want about how much you know and where you've worked and how good you are, but you'll be found out within the hour. As a chef, I want to be able to fire you right now. I don't want to give you a written warning and another next week. I know already you're not making it. That's a terrible thing to say, but it's true. Unfortunately, job security in the restaurant business often translates to mediocrity.

Certain chefs are able to be enlightened managers. They want to create a certain type of work environment that encourages, enlightens, and empowers. Maybe it's the Joe Torre school of management. Meaning, if you're leaving the kitchen and you say, "Good night chef," and he doesn't say good night back, that will be all you need to try double hard the next day. What frightens me is when it becomes managerial doublespeak. It's just meaningless psychobabble. I used to have to sit at these meetings and fill out forms, and I'd be, "Half our kitchen is illegal, have you noticed?" It could sure break a mood.

DON'T EAT FISH ON MONDAY is going to be on my tombstone. I wrote the piece that *Kitchen Confidential* was based on originally for the *New York Press,* figuring I'd get a hundred bucks for it and a free paper and that a few friends in the business would be entertained. I spoke in the same voice and the same way, as if I was, after a few beers, talking to my cooks after work, with the hope of outraging slightly and provoking any civilians who might possibly be listening in at other tables. That was very much the tone. But the *New York Press* kept bumping me from week to week to week, and so I put it in an envelope and sent it to *The New Yorker* one January. I was filleting salmon in Les Halles, still working the line, as I worked the line during the entire writing of *Kitchen Confidential,* when I got the call. "This is David Remnick. We're going to take the piece." I know who David Remnick is. I read *The New Yorker.* You know, I was pretty damn impressed and happy about it. But it never really occurred to me that it was going to go any further. I said, well, a lot more people, a lot more serious people are going to be reading this piece than I imagined. I really didn't know what to make of it. I really didn't think beyond that, and it was pretty much overnight from that point.

I was in Japan advising for Les Halles—we had a Les Halles out there briefly, when the article came out, and I got a fax offering me a book deal, saying, "Bloomsbury says they'll pay you X amount of dollars for any nonfiction project you'd care to write." Now I knew what had brought me to their attention. I knew what story I had to tell.

Again, I was given an opportunity to step up, just as you do in a restaurant. I was moving from salad to sauté, and I was determined not to screw it up. And then I just didn't think beyond what I didn't want it to be—I didn't want any cooks or chefs who read the book to say this is BS.

I never had the luxury of spending lazy afternoons staring at the ceiling thinking, what would American readers like? I just wrote the book. I had to be in at eight every morning. I was running a restaurant. I was working lunch. I had to set up my station and work the sauté station, and then hang around at night. I was expediting. I just didn't have the time to think about all the reasons why I wouldn't or couldn't or shouldn't be writing a book. I woke up a few hours earlier and wrote for as long as I could, did the best I could, and it was done. It's a good business model, I found.

I've been on the road constantly since September 2004. I've either been taping a segment for my TV shows, *A Cook's Tour* and *No Reservations*, or on a book tour or promoting the shows around the country. My business model is still pretty simple. I show up, just like in a restaurant. I'm going to show up on time every day and do the very best I can. I will know who I am and what I am capable of. I'm capable of loyalty, of hard work, of being reasonably true to myself. I'm not going to sit there thinking, well, what will they think about me? Because, as a chef, you want the loyalty and dedication of your cooks.

Whether or not they like you is another matter. You want them to know you're fair. I don't need to be loved.

I travel with two shooters, two camera people with small digital cameras, a director who also carries a camera, and an assistant producer, so we're like Spinal Tap or a band on a concert tour. Whenever we use that term *organic,* as in, "Yes, this will be an organic episode," that means we really don't have a plan. What French chefs call *system D*. I once asked a French chef what *system D* meant, and he finally explained it to me. "You've seen that show *MacGyver*? We're just making it up."

Through the shows, I have gotten to see part of the world that I never thought I would ever have the opportunity to see. I regularly find myself in situations where I'm pinching myself, saying, "I can't believe I'm here seeing this."

Once you smell Vietnam it's very hard to go back to your old life. I wrote at the end of *Kitchen Confidential* that I will always live in New York City—I don't know whether that's true anymore. There's a certain focus in my life to spend as much time as possible in Southeast Asia. For me there's no assimilating there. It's not like I will find a home in Asia. It's a place that was always there waiting for me. For any chef of any background who goes to the central fish market in Tokyo for the first time, there is a great awakening that occurs, a terrifying realization that there are more primary colors than you thought existed. It's a devastating experience for anyone who's serious about food. And it's much the same when you encounter Singapore, Shanghai, or Hong Kong. You realize, wow, I was absolutely certain that New York was the center of the world and now I'm not so sure. I got raised expectations in Asia, different expectations. New York is not enough. But I'm an adaptable guy. I always like to think that I could end up back on the sauté station if it all falls apart.

The truth is it's been a long time since I cooked in a restaurant kitchen. It's been about five years since I was of any use in the day-to-day operations at Les Halles. That being said, I was a lot more comfortable in my own skin then, as a chef, than as the food persona I have become. I knew exactly what I had to do every day. I could absolutely control my work environment. So my connection to Les Halles offers me the vicarious thrill of being out of the kitchen and yet still having the advantage of slipping back in, at least to soak up the atmosphere. I have a sense of guilt and shame at having left a kitchen that I loved and where I was relentlessly successful and busy and cooking the type of food I should have been cooking my whole career. I have a sense of family there, and we share a world-view of food. But they don't need me cooking or providing any kind of guidance for the kitchen. Carlos runs that kitchen and runs it brilliantly.

I'm not only not cooking, but I'm so pathetic that I need to hang out at the restaurant to just kind of feel that buzz again. I need to be in some way a part of it. There's no more enveloping and comfortable feeling than knowing that you belong in a restaurant, and sitting at the bar after a busy Saturday night with your cooks. So I still swim freely in that pond, and my only real friends are, in fact, restaurant people, and I don't expect that will change. We share certain character traits. First, incredible strength. Not just physical strength but strength of character, meaning you can endure everything it's going to take to get where you want to be. A sense of humor is hugely important. You have to let a lot of soul-destroying moments and tiny humiliations and disappointments roll off your back. So these are the people who keep me sane. There's always somebody who's going to say, "I hope you don't think for a second that you're hot shit, because you wrote a book and you've got a TV show." It's nice to have people remind you of that. And cooks are people who will.

Tom Colicchio

Tom Colicchio started his career in Elizabeth, New Jersey, where he was born, then moved to New York City to gain experience at The Quilted Giraffe, Gotham Bar and Grill, Rakel, and Mondrian. He later opened Gramercy Tavern and the first Craft, starting a group that has grown to include Craft Steak, Craftbar, 'Wichcraft, all in New York City, as well as a Craft Steak and 'Wichcraft in Las Vegas. Colicchio has been awarded Chef of the Year from *Bon Appétit* and the Food Network, as well as receiving the James Beard KitchenAid Cookbook Award for his first cookbook, *Think Like a Chef.*

Both of my parents loved to cook. My mother did the tried-and-true stuff—meatballs, manicotti, Sunday gravy— whereas my father was more experimental. I grew up eating good food—it was just a given. I liked reading food magazines such as *Gourmet* and *Cuisine,* which I found in my cousin Patty's hair salon. *Cuisine* is defunct now, but back in the mid-seventies it was cutting-edge stuff. I saw an ad in the back of *Gourmet* for Pierre Au Tunnel, which sounded like the absolute definition of sophisticated French dining, so I saved up and took my high school girlfriend there. Fancy French food—it didn't get more radical than that for an Italian kid from Elizabeth, New Jersey.

Looking back, I see that I was the classic ADD kid—restless, easily distracted. I was bright enough, but school bored me and my grades reflected that. One day my father came home from his job as a corrections officer with a bunch of cookbooks he'd picked up en route. I flipped through them, immediately interested. The one that really caught my eye was Jacques Pépin's *La Technique*. It was a very visual book—filled with photos of Jacques's own hands working with food. His proficiency with a knife intrigued me, and I decided to teach myself knife skills. I started on celery, because it was so cheap. I could cut and throw it out, cut and throw it out. Once I nailed that, I pressed forward with the book, making chicken stock. The book said consommé was one of the hardest things to get right. I regarded that as a challenge, so of course I taught myself to make consommé.

Growing up, my family belonged to a swim club in Clark, New Jersey. The summer I was fourteen I got hired to scoop ice cream in the club's snack bar. Soon I was working the grill, and the owner was scooping ice cream. I became known as the kid who cooked. The food was basic—grilled cheese sandwiches and burgers—but making them taught me how to use heat. When a Burger King opened in my neighborhood, a long line formed on the sidewalk, but I was the one they hired. I found that I liked cooking as a job—I was good at it, and I liked having money in my pocket.

I didn't consider cooking a career until the day my dad said, "You really should think about being a chef." That made sense to me, and I agreed (surprising him, no doubt). My father and I drove up to The Culinary Institute of America in Hyde Park, New York, where we learned that working in a few restaurants was a prerequisite to acceptance. (Burger King and the snack bar didn't count.) Thus began my restaurant career. My father had a friend in the refrigeration business who had installed some units in a new place, and he got me in.

From that point on I kept working in restaurants. Some of the cooks I'd work with would say, "You should go to New York." Growing up seeing the New York skyline, I felt you only got one shot over there and I wanted to be ready when I took it. Eventually I got my résumé together and shopped it around to places I'd heard of or read about. I applied to Jonathan Waxman at Jams, and Alfred Portale at The Gotham Bar and Grill. (Both are still good friends today.) But while I was still waiting to hear back from Alfred, I got a call from Barry Wine at The Quilted Giraffe. This was pretty exciting; I'd read about the place in *Cuisine*.

I got the job, and The Quilted Giraffe became one of my formative work experiences. The restaurant was known for its beggar's purses, basically a crêpe filled with caviar, tied with a blanched chive—an archetype of nouvelle cuisine. The dish was famous, and we made them all day long, but there was a lot more going on at The Quilted Giraffe than that. Barry would come in on Monday mornings with incredible produce from his farm upstate, and we would just start creating. Barry wasn't afraid to spend money on training, on silverware and glassware, and maintaining an excellent physical space.

The kitchen was fantastic. All this made a huge impression on me. This was the very dawn of the celebrity chef era; Alfred Portale was becoming really successful, and Charlie Palmer and David Burke were getting ready to make a splash, and Wayne Nish and David Kinch were in the kitchen with me. It was an exciting time to be cooking in New York City.

One guy whose reputation was soaring was Thomas Keller, at Rakel. I went to work for him as a sous-chef in 1987. Thomas did something in his kitchen that I found fascinating: he talked food. It wasn't that other subjects weren't welcome; they just didn't come up. The ingredients coming in were so exceptional, it got us excited about the possibilities. Thomas was a generous collaborator. "I have lamb shanks coming in," someone would say, or "we could pair this with that," and Thomas would be open to the ideas that emerged from those discussions. I remember a party of twelve coming in, and Thomas said, "Let's make them some foie gras." I took the whole lobe of foie gras and was about to put it into the pan, and Thomas asked, "What are you doing?" "I'm just going to roast the whole lobe," I said. He looked at me and asked, "Is that going to work?" "I think so," I said. "It had better." That was the kind of environment Thomas created: no holds barred.

I made the leap from sous-chef to chef at a restaurant called 40 Main Street, in Milburn, New Jersey. It was a chance for me to step away from the intense spotlight of New York City. At first, all I did was a retread of the dishes I'd learned at The Quilted Giraffe. About two months into it, I said to myself, "I need to stop playing it safe, and develop a style of my own." It was a considerable risk—after all, it's easier to succeed copying other people than risk failing as yourself. That was a big decision, because it would begin the process of discovering my own culinary voice.

With time, the confidence I developed led me back to New York, where I became the chef at Mondrian, the restaurant where I would first make my name in the city, and also learn a thing or two about restaurant economics. The restaurant's investors had spent $3.5 million on the building, and had agreed to an exorbitant $34,000 monthly rent for an 80-seat place. This was not good restaurant math. Even at capacity every night of the week, we could only operate at a loss. Eventually I sat down with the investors, a group of Morgan Stanley bankers, and said, "Let's close it. How much is it going to cost for a Chapter Eleven?" They threw out a figure like a hundred thousand dollars, and I said, "How about we take half of that and just pay off our suppliers the best we can." I knew I was going to open another restaurant, and I didn't want to jeopardize those relationships. Bob Scott, who was the majority shareholder, and is still my friend and business partner, said, "Go ahead and do it." We explained the situation to our suppliers and paid them each fifty cents on the dollar, which was a good deal more than the ten cents on the dollar they can usually hope for.

I met Danny Meyer at the Aspen Food & Wine Festival in 1991, the year that Michael Romano and I were named *Food & Wine*'s Rising Star Chefs. Danny was a fan of Mondrian, as I was of Union Square Cafe, and we each enjoyed a reputation for doing things right. The day before I closed Mondrian, I called him and said, "I'm calling to let you know that I'm closing." And he said, "Thanks,

but why are you telling me?" I said, "We should do something together." Well, it's one thing to know a person's reputation and another to know the person, so we decided to take a trip together to Italy. By the time we got home we not only knew we had enough in common to open a restaurant, we had the idea sketched out on a napkin.

The goal was to update a classic restaurant form. But what should it be? The bar and grill had been done as well as it could ever be at the Gotham. Danny had already revived and expanded upon the idea of a café at Union Square. How about a tavern? We did some research about taverns and learned that historically they had been the central gathering place for a community. A place to eat well and connect with others. The idea of updating and reinterpreting the classic tavern felt right. We learned that the word *Gramercy* derives from a Dutch word meaning crooked river—Gramercy Park is named for a small river that once ran through the area. At one point I threw out "Crooked River Tavern." Nah, too gimmicky. We kept coming back to Gramercy Park, near where the new place would be opening, and decided to call it Gramercy Tavern.

Danny and I were both terrified on the day Gramercy Tavern

opened, especially because of the media firestorm that went along with it. But, luckily, the restaurant was a success from the start. For one, the underlying math made sense: The dining room sat 130 diners, plus 60 at the bar, as well as a private room that could accommodate between 12 and 22 diners—all for a rent of $8,000 a month. But it was more than figures. From the beginning, Gramercy Tavern was a partnership of equals, which made for strong collaborative energy. Both Danny and I brought investors to the deal, making us answerable to each other and to shareholders who trusted us. We had many common experiences, both professional and personal: Both of our fathers passed away from lung cancer right at the same time, and we both became fathers for the first time a month apart. Even years later, when we both owned other restaurants, we knew that the only two people who could screw things up at Gramercy Tavern were the two of us, and we resolved not to let that happen. When I eventually sold my share of the restaurant to Danny, it was for the same reason we'd started Gramercy in the first place, to continue to grow and create something unique.

Craft is very much a New York restaurant in that it started out because of the concerns of a co-op board. The president of a co-op around the corner from Gramercy Tavern contacted me wanting to know about restaurant issues like garbage collection. I said, "Why are you asking?" And he said, "We have someone who wants to build a restaurant on the ground floor." I answered their questions, but as time went by I didn't see any construction at that address. So I called the guy and asked if I could look at the space. "No, no, that person fell through, but we have another person lined up," he told me. Again, time went by and I saw nothing happening. Finally he called me. "Okay, let's talk." By then I think he understood that New York is full of people who are in the restaurant business up until the moment they have to sign a lease.

But opening Craft wasn't just about the space. It had a lot to do with how I was developing as a chef. I think young cooks believe that you reach some kind of plateau as a chef where you say, "Okay, I've got my style, I've got my restaurant, I can kick back now." But it doesn't really work that way. A style is an ongoing process. It evolves as the person evolves. As you work, you grow, you self-edit, and as you become more confident and assured, you self-edit some more. For me, that process became about stripping down. I found that I was increasingly drawn to simplicity. I was seeing better ingredients out there than at any time before, and I found myself reluctant to overwhelm those ingredients with "art." I wanted to see how close to basic and essential food I could get. I think that's a secret fascination that we chefs have: How close to simple can we get while keeping the integrity of the dish, and keeping the integrity of that thing we've devoted our lives to perfecting, that thing called craft?

So I wanted to knock the bells and whistles off the food and get down to its essence. Peter Bentel and his partners at Bentel and Bentel understood exactly what I was talking about, and reflected this in their design; we used stone and cold-rolled steel, without the finishes that would have obscured the materials. We stripped terra cotta off of the brick columns, leaving them exposed in their natural state. When we welded the wine cabinet, we didn't polish the seam away—we wanted its workmanship to remain visible. There was beauty in the way it was crafted.

The success of Craft has enabled us to open other restaurants, and each in its own way reflects the culinary philosophy of the original. We have Craftbar, which is more casual—a place to kick back with a glass of wine and a plate of pasta. Gamal Aziz, the president of the MGM Hotel in Las Vegas, encouraged us to open a steakhouse there. We called it Craftsteak, and now we have a second one here in New York City. Sisha Ortuzar, who worked as a cook for me for years, came up with the idea of applying the Craft philosophy to sandwiches. That became 'Wichcraft, and we've since opened a few, both in New York and Las Vegas. I loved the idea of giving a talented employee a chance to grow and become a partner, while staying true to Craft's central vision. It felt right at the time, and still does, with each new venture.

There's a certain mark that each chef has in his or her kitchen. I cook things a certain way. I use heat a certain way—very slow and controlled, which takes a lot of skill and teases out the maximum flavor from ingredients. I braise a lot and I do that a certain way; I want the result to be incredibly lush and decadent. Even something like a mushroom—I have my own way of dealing with mushrooms, tomatoes, grains, and fish. It's very specific, and there is no margin for error because we're showcasing food in its simplest and truest form. My cooks learn this approach and repeat it in each of the restaurants. But when you're cooking for hundreds on a given night, there's a bigger picture at play: production. Understanding how to put a dish into production in a busy kitchen is one of the most important things a restaurant chef can do. It's all about organization and preparation, but not overpreparation. My idea of a well-run kitchen is one that has figured out what can be done in advance that won't be detrimental to the final outcome of a dish. And that's the moment we have to prepare for. Everything else is *à la minute*.

I don't like being called "Chef." In my kitchens, I ask my cooks to call me Tom. I think it relaxes them—in a good way. In my twenties I was more of a screamer—I let the pressure get to me. But over time I learned that when you're yelling, that's all people can hear. They're not hearing the message, and now they're tense on top of everything else. There are different ways of lighting a fire under people. Most people are curious, and most people want to do their best. If someone is doing something wrong, you'll get a better result by saying, "This is how you do it. Watch." A well-run kitchen has to allow time for those moments, too.

Every so often I hear reference to my "restaurant empire." I don't like the word *empire*; empires tend to be evil. This work we're doing is not an unstoppable march. We don't just open these places. We labor over each one, spending months—even years—in discussion and planning. To me, each one of my restaurants says something and stands for something I believe in. If it's a sandwich at 'Wichcraft, I want it to be made of the best food you can put between two slices of really great bread. If it's a mushroom at Craft, I want you to eat it and think, that's the best a mushroom can taste.

Some people seem to have reservations about whether chefs should have multiple restaurants. I guess because it violates the romantic ideal of what a chef should be: one man laboring behind the stove. But that's a myth even with just one restaurant. Restaurants are collaborations of many talented individuals, centered around the vision and techniques of one person. So when people ask me how it is I can open other places, I tell them I don't see other businesses standing still. I won't ever feel I have to apologize for looking after my family, my restaurants, or my staff. There, that's how we lay it out in New Jersey.

Cat Cora

Cat Cora is the first and only female Iron Chef on the Food Network. She also co-hosts *Melting Pot*. She was born in Jackson, Mississippi, and grew up immersed in both a Greek and Southern food culture. She spent time in New York City studying under Anne Rosenzweig of Arcadia and Larry Forgione of An American Place, and worked in France learning from Georges Blanc and Roger Vergé. She then moved to Northern California to work at Napa Valley's Bistro Don Giovanni. She is the author of the cookbooks *Cat Cora's Kitchen* and *Cooking from the Hip*.

I don't know if it's the heat, but the South has produced great blues men, great writers, and great cooks. The Mississippi I grew up in really brought out the creative energy of people. We didn't have New York City and all these fine things at our fingertips. We created them ourselves. We created entertainment through writing, music, and food.

My grandfather opened restaurants in the Delta. He had coffee shops—actually "diners" are what they called them—in places like Greenville and Lexington. He would get up in the morning and run them from morning till midnight. That's what he could afford to open.

87

He was an immigrant, straight from Skopelos, Greece, to Ellis Island to Jackson.

People find it bizarre that there are so many Greeks in the South. But there are a lot more than people think, because of the climate. The fishing industry in the Gulf Coast attracted many. And it was a lot cheaper to open a diner in the South than in New York or Chicago. So a lot of Greeks did settle in the South and they started diners and Greek Orthodox churches. Greeks were often the first people to open white tablecloth restaurants, so in terms of fine dining they upped the ante a bit. Most of the fine-dining establishments in Jackson were owned by Greeks. My godfather had made some money in real estate and he opened a place called the Shamrock, which was the first place to sell frozen pizza. With the money he made he was able to open up a fine-dining place. I guess an Irish-named, Greek-owned pizza joint was a lucky thing.

Growing up Greek in the South certainly made one feel different. When I was young I'd wonder, "Why are we having steamed artichokes and olive oil instead of fried okra like the rest of the kids?" Now I know it was because we were lucky, but back then you thought you were just a little bit weird. When Easter came along we were dyeing Easter eggs red when everyone else had pastel blues and pinks. On Thanksgiving we'd have corn pudding and turkey on the table *with* dolmades, spanakopita, feta cheese, and kalamata olives. Other than that it was your typical southern childhood. Pitchers of tea brewing in the sun, fresh lemonade for special guests, and lots of hearing "Don't be going in and out so much."

I had plenty of crazy notions. I wanted to be a veterinarian. But I also wanted to be a horse jockey because I was kind of petite. My favorite thing to do was tea parties. I'd wear white gloves and I'd put on little dresses and I would bake cookies that were squeezed out of an old-fashioned aluminum tube. I would make my grandparents sit down, or my parents—it didn't matter; I just needed an audience.

Later, when I was eleven or twelve, my brothers and I would help my uncle at his restaurant. We'd set the tables or do little odd jobs, and he'd give us a dollar or two. I wanted to be like him. I wanted to have a restaurant. I thought they were incredible places. We'd often go to a place called Angelo's, and just walking in there was cool; it was kind of sultry and kind of loungy, with red booths and big steaks. There was something about the energy of restaurants that I found fascinating.

I think when you grow up in a small place like Jackson there is really an added challenge to making it, to really getting out and into the world and creating your own space out there. My parents were hugely supportive of anything I might decide to do. I got a degree in exercise physiology and a minor in biology, with nutrition studies on the side, and I did cardiac rehab during my internship. But then I decided to go to culinary school, and I attended The Culinary Institute of America. While I was there I worked at the Beekman Arms, under Larry Forgione and Melissa Kelly, and I interned at Arcadia, under Anne Rosenzweig. In Arcadia it was interesting to work in a female-run kitchen because though you'll always be judged by whether you can do it or not, there's something about a female-run kitchen that is more nurturing.

I'm not sure I'd call the next place I went to nurturing—I went to France. I'm just a total overachiever and sometimes I get myself into situations that I go, "What did I do to myself? How did I get here?"

But going to France had always been something I'd wanted to do, and I set about now trying to do it. I got a package together and sent out ten applications. In quick succession I got eight rejections back. Two accepted me: Georges Blanc and Roger Vergé. I said, "Well, I can't choose." How can you choose between those two? So I took both, and two weeks after graduating I was on a plane going, "What have I gotten myself into?"

Working in French kitchens is a tremendous experience. It's very hard, very competitive, and it can feel very foreign. But it also gives you tremendous confidence to know that you can handle it. I wanted to see these kitchens firsthand, because if you don't, it's hard to understand how everything they do strives for perfection. They have to be that way; their reputation is everything. Still, when I was dropped off on a rainy March day in a dormitory in Vonnas, where Georges Blanc is located, it was suddenly very real. All night I was going, "Okay, I'm in France." I got up early and walked to the restaurant. I met some people and I thought, "Okay, I can do this." You're psyching yourself out because you know it's going to be intense. Finally I walked into the kitchen. They put me on garnishes, and I started.

As soon as I got back I sort of started a process of not forgetting what I learned in France but perhaps diminishing the colossal influence of France. Melissa Kelly, Larry Forgione's protégée called me and said, "I'm opening this place called The Old Chatham Sheepherding Company," and she said, "Just come see it. Come see what we're doing here. I'd love for you to be my opening sous-chef." So I drove to Old Chatham and saw her and the space, saw everything, and knew that it was just going to be the two of us cooking in the kitchen together with a couple of helpers. We were going to be changing the menu every day based on what's fresh and seasonal, getting products in from all over, and eventually building our own garden. Price, her fiancé, was the bread baker, and we'd be getting fresh lamb and cheeses from the farm. So it was just one of those very organic opportunities I couldn't pass up. It was just too wonderful.

It was great working with Melissa because she wants as close to perfection as possible, but it wasn't French. I was able to be a part of everything, from the ground up and also, then, helping Melissa to create this magical place that people could come to. And also, it was just us, so we didn't have the whole brigade system. It wasn't so formal. We got to make our own creations out of whatever was in season. There was a lot of creative process there that I didn't get to have in France, where I was just a pure student.

But the greatest moment of liberation may have come while cooking for Jacques Pépin. I was chef at Bistro Don Giovanni in the Napa Valley. The Mondavis always came in. Robert always came to the back and said, "Cat, what's your fish of the day?" That was his favorite, the whole fish. One night they brought in Jacques. I think it was a Monday night, so everybody was gone. It was just me, so I'm calling the owners: "Oh, my God. Jacques is here. What do I do? What do I make?" And so, of course, instinctively as a young chef, I started going down the French path but then I went, "No, no, no, no. This is what we do here. This is my soul food. This is what I'm going to do," and I didn't make that drastic mistake that it would have been. So I sent out many of my favorites and some of the creations that I loved, and he actually said, "You know, can you come out and sit down with me for a little while?" and so I came out, and we must have talked for an hour. He gave me so much advice, was so mentoring, I was just blown away.

And two weeks later I got a letter, it was a copy of a letter Jacques had taken the time to write to the James Beard House, saying, "I just want you to know I was just on a visit to San Francisco and Napa Valley, and I ate at many restaurants," he said, "but one restaurant stuck out." And he said, "It was Bistro Don Giovanni, and the chef there is Cat Cora, and you must immediately invite her to come and cook at the James Beard House. It was the most fantastic meal that I've had in a long time." And to me, I was just—I was crying, and I had this letter, and I'm like, "Oh, my God," you know. I just could not believe it. It was one of the first huge highlights of my career.

I'd always been curious about TV and who was on. Usually it was Julia Child. I also remember watching an old Cajun guy, the Cookin' Cajun, who was hilarious. He wore suspenders, drank a little bit, poured some in the pot, that kind of thing. I got a call to do a local show in San Francisco called *Bay Café*. I sent a tape of that to the Food Network, and about two weeks later it landed in the right hands and someone called me. I did a couple of guest appearances, then a couple more, and then I got an offer to audition for a show. It happened pretty fast. That was probably 1999, and the show was *Melting Pot*. That started my journey in television.

I was in New York doing the *Today* show, and Bruce Sidell called me from Food Network and said, "What do you think about being the first female Iron Chef?" I didn't even think. I just said, "Yes." I just knew that for that instant it sounded right, and I jumped at the opportunity. I felt I had all the tools. I could cook. I had loved competition ever since I played fast-pitch softball as a girl, and I knew about cardiac rehab—just in case Bobby or Mario needed some help.

It is the biggest pressurized situation that I think out of all the appearances we do in front of thousands of people and is one of the most stressful things we can do in our career. I get asked a lot if it's real. And it really is. That hour that you see us cooking, that is real time. They don't stop the clock. We are the Iron Chefs: (a) we have to live up to that, and (b) we are also going up against some of our top colleagues in the industry. Everybody comes to win, and the chefs are really competitive.

We truly don't know the secret ingredient. That's the fact of the matter, so we prepare with our sous-chefs that are going to be on with us. We can say to them, "Okay, if it's fish, we're going to do this. If it's shellfish . . ." and you have to really work on those kinds of things and just do your best, because chefs have a repertoire. When you get to that level, you should be able to pull recipes out of your hat and dishes out of your hat, and that's really what a lot of it is, you know, improvisation. Once they lift the lid, we have about five minutes to go, "Okay, now that we know it's a vegetable," this is what we're going to do." It's a bit like calling a play in football. "Okay, we know it's shrimp. Play twenty-two. Hut!"

People think if you're doing television you're not really cooking. I cook all the time. I cook at demos, I go to appearances. Purists say, "Well, in the old days it wasn't like that." I think it's wonderful that we can go into the households of the people who are our fans and say, "Hey, how are you today? We're going to cook some." What I think is a mistake is starting out on a culinary career with the goal of being on television. You have to be much more focused on what is real and tangible in cooking. Work your station and study someone else's. When chefs get in the weeds and need someone, that should be you. When the sauté cook doesn't show up and you have to take over the station when before you'd maybe been placed on salads, then get in there and do it. Prove yourself. When the last order gets spiked and the dust settles, you'll be looked at differently and you'll think of yourself differently, too.

My partner and I have a young son, Zoran. I work out of my home when I'm home, and at a certain point in the day I say, "Okay, this is my family time." I really learned quickly when we had Zoran that you have to set your boundaries. If you don't, you're really missing out. I don't want to get older and not know my kids. I'm also the founder and president of Chefs for Humanity, which is like a Doctors Without Borders type of nonprofit, both for culinary professionals and for people who have an affinity for food and wine and want to be part of it. We don't exclude anyone.

I had a plan to do something like a culinary peace corps, and then

Hurricane Katrina hit. We went to Gulfport, Mississippi, and we were feeding three thousand to five thousand people a day. Ming Tsai, executives from Food Network, Charlie Ayers, local chefs, and others on our chef's council came down, and we were just cooking masses of food. There were truckloads of frozen foods, but people who are used to putting a family dinner on the table every evening don't even know where to start with that kind of volume. They were so relieved when we got there. We went into the trucks, took inventory, and started cooking using all the products, and making sure all the sanitary issues were taken care of. I didn't realize just how much chefs and culinary professionals are needed in disaster situations. When people have nothing else, food is one thing they can look forward to.

When I was fifteen I wrote a business plan, for my godfather, of the restaurant I wanted to have. I didn't really know what it would look like. I just knew I wanted it to be called Spiro, after my dad, which is still what I want today. That has never left. And I still want it to be very much about my Mediterranean roots. I think to be successful in food you have to come from a place in your heart. If you're not coming from there, chances are you may not be successful. That's my place. I'm a chef before I'm a TV personality or a cookbook author. Before I'm anything else, I'm a chef. That's my heart and soul. So I hope that soon I'll actually be able to open Spiro, the restaurant I've dreamt of for so long. I kind of did things a little backward; everything else came first. But I'm very excited by the prospect. I can't wait to get behind the stove.

Robert
Del Grande

After receiving a Ph.D. in biochemistry, Robert Del Grande has continued in a similar mind-set, experimenting with the flavors of the Southwest. He is currently the executive chef and partner of Café Annie, in Houston, which has received *Food & Wine*'s award for Best Restaurant in Houston. Del Grande also created Café Express, which offers "good food fast," and Taco Milagro, his interpretation of Tex-Mex. He has received numerous culinary awards and honors.

I was born in San Francisco and spent twenty-one years there and in Burlingame, south of the city. My parents were both schoolteachers in public schools. My mother taught English. My father taught science and then took over the local NPR station, so that was always on in our house. Even though I was a teenager in the city during the so-called crazy sixties, my parents took the rational approach to the times. Essentially it was, "Don't be an idiot, if you want to drink have a drink at home, and whatever time you come in don't creep in or we'll mistake you for a burglar." The one rule was that my sister and I had to be home for dinner, which even then was a rule I wanted to keep.

My mother took her cooking very seriously. She would write out all the good recipes from magazines and books on three-by-five cards, which she kept in a drawer, and she had them filed practically on the Dewey decimal system. Chicken casserole came before chicken Kiev. Years later, when I was at graduate school, I would write home asking for recipes for certain dishes. She would write out the recipe, and a few days later a three-by-five card would arrive in the mail. I still think that if a recipe can't fit on a three-by-five card, it's too long.

If my parents were having people over, my siblings and I were the guinea pigs. My mother would work away on a dish, and then she would let us try it. I loved the whole idea of working on a dish. "That's so good. How did you make that?" I would ask, often the first person to praise a new creation. Those were real dinner parties, not "Why don't you come over and we'll hang out." Hostesses ruled. Gentlemen wore a tie and jacket. You had proper cocktails, and even a modicum of service, since my sister and I would often help serve.

With the kind of situation I had at home, I was in no rush to go away to college, so I studied chemistry and biology at the University of San Francisco. Then I had to decide what I wanted to do. I didn't want to go to medical school, since I didn't like hospitals. As an undergraduate in that position you're taking all the introductory courses and so forth, and when I'd go to talk to the professors, I walked past all the graduate-level labs, and it looked intriguing. They were doing the real cool stuff, where the answers weren't in the back of the book. So I got a job in one of those labs, saying I'd wash glassware if they let me help out every once in a while. A lot of people started in the restaurant business washing dishes. I guess the beginning of my path started with washing glassware in a research lab.

I knew that straight biology wasn't for me; I didn't want to be running up and down mountains looking for birds. But biochemistry was a good marriage of biology and chemistry. For my postgraduate studies, I got accepted to UC Riverside, where there was a professor working on protein synthesis, a subject I was particularly interested in. On the day I left home, my mother packed me up with stuff I would need: I had a roasting pan, platters, and even a Presto Pot. I also had my treasured Martin D35 acoustic guitar, which I'd bought with money I'd made working at Baskin-Robbins. I got all that into a forest green Ford Pinto, which I used to call the Land Rocket, for its ability to get from zero to sixty in no less than an hour. I had installed an FM radio in the car because everyone who was cool listened to FM. The format was really loose. The stations had no commercials. You'd hear some shuffling papers. "Oh, by the way, this was brought to you by ... where's that piece of paper again?" The guy would kind of read it. "Oh, yeah, Hills Brothers coffee. Great coffee." That's the kind of thing I would have been hearing as I left San Francisco.

In Riverside, I lived by myself for a few months, and then some guys I knew wanted me to get a house with them. The one rule was that we had to eat dinner together every night. This wasn't going to be one of *those* houses, where people just came and went. We decided that the three of us would take turns with the cooking. They cooked the first two nights; when dinner was ready you kind of loaded down your plate and sat down. I cooked the last night. I made a roast chicken, which was one of the few things I knew how to do, and I put it on a platter and brought it to the table, just as my mother did. They sort of went, "Holy smoke," in unison. Then they said, "You cook, and we'll clean up," and for the next five years I did.

At first I was a very serious student. Perhaps even a little grim. I was convinced that it was undignified for a graduate student to be having fun. Consequently, I spent a lot of time at the library and at bookstores. That's how you acquired knowledge. If you had a question, you went to the library. You went to the bookstore. Literature contained stuff. Well, protein synthesis can only hold your attention for so long, and eventually I wandered over to the cooking shelves. At the UC Riverside Library, I bought some early cookbooks, such as James Beard's *American Cookery*. I also I bought Jacques Pépin's *La Technique*. Being in Southern California, I was used to seeing Los Angeles constantly abbreviated to L.A., so I first picked up the book thinking it was going to tell me how they did things over in Los Angeles.

At the university library I also got to know Mimi, my future wife. She worked the three p.m.-to-midnight shift. So we'd go out at midnight, which was fine because by then Riverside would have cooled down a little. There was a Howard Johnson just down from the campus, so that was good for late-night breakfast. Mimi had just gotten back from Spain when I met her, so for a while it was, "Let's get a bottle of sherry and sit under the trees." I can still tell someone's just come back from Spain when they say, "Hey, would you like some sherry?" We were gastronomes with modest budgets. We'd go to a little place in Los Angeles, or even Laguna Beach, where there were cute restaurants along the water. I got interested in wine, and we'd go to one of the first Trader Joe's and get something interesting. I would cook dinner and we'd drink the bottle of wine. Everything seemed good at the time.

Until, that is, Mimi moved to Houston. Her sister Candice had married a Houstonian, Lonnie Schiller, and they were starting a restaurant. At first they'd been doing marketing for a real estate group. One of their developments was a strip mall just west of the Galleria that was going to have a restaurant, and Candice and Lonnie decided to rent it themselves. So they started Café Annie in 1980. The initial look was French bistro, a Parisian-looking place. It was a long cigar box shape, with a black-and-white floor, and mirrors and some brass. Candice wanted to name it something that had some weight and sophistication. They chose Café Annie as a temporary thing, just to file some paperwork, but by the time the painter showed up to do the sign they hadn't thought of anything else, so that's what it remained.

It had been open about six months by the time I decided to go see Mimi. My professor at Riverside knew somebody at the Medical Center in Houston, and I thought I could always get a post-doc there. So I moved in much the same way I'd left San Francisco. I loaded up a VW Sirocco just as I'd loaded the Land Rocket: pots, platters, Presto Pot, and Martin guitar, and in June '81 drove from Riverside to Houston.

I was a food maniac by then, and by the end of the first week I'd asked if I could help in the kitchen at Café Annie. No one saw any reason why not. There was a French chef at the restaurant and he prepared food that was in the French bistro style, with a few American dishes scattered around. You could, for example, order escargot in the traditional little clay pots or a nice crab salad. I thought I would learn a lot from him. But pretty early on one of the French waiters took me aside and said, "Hey, let me just give you some advice. These guys, they worked at a burger shack in Paris, and they come over here with their French accent and all of a sudden they're French chefs. Don't think they know everything that's going on. They're in America now, so they're French chefs."

Pretty soon I got to understand what he meant. I'd be talking to the chef and I'd say, "Hey, what do you think of Troisgros. What they're doing is just killer, isn't it?" He said, "Who's Troisgros?" "You know, down in Roanne." "Nah, don't know who that is." "You know Michel Guérard? He's doing this thing ..." "Don't know who that is, either." So all of a sudden I realized he didn't know anybody. He was pretty young. He liked two things, windsurfing and girls. Working in a restaurant interfered with those pursuits. I came from graduate school, where they work you like a dog, so I was used to the hours that I was soon logging in the kitchen. Next to the old Café Annie was a bookstore, and I'd scan through all their stuff and buy a cookbook. I'd read the book and explain a recipe to the crew, and if they liked it we tried it. There were a couple of guys who had worked in hotels and that wanted to do something interesting, and they started coming to me for information. I became the source of knowledge for the kitchen, even though I didn't know hardly anything. So, eventually, it did come down to who was going to follow whom. But it wasn't traumatic. The chef didn't care that much overall. I'd say, "Hey, I'm thinking

of doing this," to which he'd reply, "Great, I'm going windsurfing in Galveston and I'll be back later."

At first our atmosphere was more groundbreaking than our food. Our approach to the restaurant was that it should be fun. We were twenty-six, twenty-seven years old and we felt that the atmosphere in a restaurant shouldn't be similar to that of a funeral parlor. We weren't thinking about who was sitting at which table or any of those kind of considerations. This drove some of the older European waiters crazy. People would come in, announce they had a reservation, and Mimi would walk them to the edge of the dining room and say, "Where would you like to sit?" The people were astounded; the waiters, appalled. They'd say, "This is not how you run a restaurant. You

103

don't ask the guests where they would like to sit. You put them down, and you're authoritative about it." That wasn't Mimi's approach at all. She'd essentially say, "Where would you like to be happy?"

Our culinary development was a question of outgrowing the French. That doesn't mean rejecting the French. I can use the Troisgros brothers as an example of what I mean, since at the time I had a particular fascination with them. Jean Troisgros struck me as the ideal chef: smart, dynamic, intelligent, and good at tennis. Pierre Troisgros was the soul of France. So in that situation, at first you want to do their recipes. Then you realize that copying nouvelle cuisine in Texas is a little uphill. You know, just a little uphill. So then you get to a deeper question than duplication. You ask, "What is it that makes them so good?" Well, one of those things is that they use what's around them. It's Roanne cuisine more than French cuisine. So eventually you get to a moment where you want to cook with ingredients that are close to you, your kitchen, and your backdoor. The irony is, when you stop looking to Roanne and set your sights locally, you're getting much closer to the Troisgros philosophy.

At some stage the chefs who would eventually develop southwestern cuisine kind of came to that understanding together. At one point we all understood—we were all thinking the same thing—that the best we could ever manage would be an excellent copy, while waiting for the next idea to come out of France. It would be like being in a tribute band: we'd put out our version of the hits and then be in the back with the gang, eating tacos and enchiladas and stuff. Well, at a certain stage the light goes off. "Hey, maybe we should cook what we like. How much future can there really be in imitating the French the best you can?"

Without wanting to be overly dramatic about it, I will say that for us it all came down to a rabbit dish. That was the crossroads dish of Café Annie. We'd buy these rabbits because that was a French thing to do. We took the back end, the saddle and the legs, and prepared it as we'd see in books—with mustard and so forth, in a French style. Then we had the front end piling up. One day I decided to braise the front legs up in a kind of Mexican style, as a meal for the staff. So I cooked them in sauce and I pulled the meat off, and we made enchiladas out of it and used the sauce for the stock, and everyone was eating, going, "God, these are unbelievable. These are unbelievable."

A few days later I put it on as a special. Now, I love the front of the house but they're with you as long as it's working. And I don't blame them at all; they're right there on the front lines. Well, the rabbit wasn't working. The service was going along, and we hadn't sold one. I asked what was going on, and they kind of looked at their shoes and said, "Well, we go to the table and say, 'And tonight for an appetizer we have a wonderful, beautiful rabbit enchilada,' and people just laugh and think that's just absurd." I was annoyed and sort of kicking the ground. And in one of those moments, I said, "Make you all a deal. They laugh, they get it free." So we gave them away free, and there was no turning back. From then on, people were calling, "I'd like to reserve two rabbit enchiladas for tonight." Now it was the loins and legs that were piling up.

That's kind of how we progressed. A lot of things we did that turned out fairly well we almost didn't do. We sort of sat around on it for a while until we got to that point of, just give it a run and see what happens. It's better to claim you never did it than never doing it and thinking you should have.

In 1989 we moved to a new location, on Post Oak Boulevard. Moving what was then a pretty well-known restaurant is hard. People say, "Don't change anything." Well, why move if you don't change anything? I liked the look of places like Tadich Grill in San Francisco, that have a classic big-city look to them. We eventually followed the same idea of the black-and-white stone floors, but we modulated it a bit, away from the French look and more toward a very subtle western grillroom. Some people still see a French look to the place.

While the move has allowed us to be more elegant—the restaurant has a lovely gray-and-beige stone floor, with African mahogany paneling and columns—we have managed to retain the spirit of the restaurant. That, for me, is the great mystery of restaurants, the feeling a place can have that you can neither control nor define. Over the years people have asked us to build another Café Annie. For me it has always come back to, if we build another one, how do I know which one's the real one and which one's the imitation?

Café Annie is home. It's the place I came to as a young man in love, in that confusing stage when your heart and your career and some big decisions are all mixed up. As a person, it helped lay a solid foundation. It's still the four of us: Candice and Lonnie, Mimi and me. As a cook, it helped me develop a style that is proud of its simplicity and authenticity, and not trying to pretend to be anything that it's not. Cooking is this amazing occupation where what you're doing can confound you; at times you don't even understand why something you just made is so good. I can only liken it to music, because the elements are similar. There are consonant flavors and dissonant flavors and harmonic relationships. And they are both similarly fleeting. You play the chord; there it goes. You cook the dish; there it goes. It makes us appreciate the moment because you can't have it back.

Todd English

Todd English started his career at La Côte Basque in New York, under Jean-Jacques Rachou, and later traveled to Italy, working in restaurants such as Dal Pescatore and Paracucchi, where he developed his unique style, drawing from his Italian experience and heritage. Once back in the United States, he started Olives, in Charlestown, Massachusetts, and later opened other locations, in New York, Las Vegas, Washington, D.C., Aspen, and Tokyo. His other restaurants include Figs, Tuscany, Bonfire, Kingfish Hall, Fish Club, Blue Zoo, and a restaurant aboard the *Queen Mary 2*. Early in his career, English was named National Rising Star Chef by the James Beard Foundation, and later received the award for Best Chef Northeast. He has been on countless television shows and is the author of three cookbooks.

When I was starting out, I didn't make the necessary pilgrimage to France. Instead, I wanted to go see what was going on in Italy. In the early eighties there were few American kids there. It was not on the charts. My Italian was limited to the six or seven words that my Italian grandmother spoke to me. Tony May, the godfather of Italian food in America, set me up there. Essentially he gave me a name and address: Signor Morini at San Domenico restaurant, in Emilia-Romagna.

109

So off I went on my journey in Italy, with one ticket, one bag, and one piece of paper.

After a day or so of planes, trains, and a lot of hand gesturing, I got to this tiny town, and of course the restaurant was closed. I knocked on the door, and a man opened it. I didn't know it was Signor Morini himself. I handed him the note that Tony May had given me. He shut the door. I'm standing outside, and I'm like, damn, I came all this way. Now what am I going to do? And then about five minutes later he opens up the door and he says, "Come in. You come in." He must have made a call to Tony. So in I went, and the first thing they do is feed you a meal. So a nice bowl of risotto. I remember everything about that meal, and it was, like, wow, this is amazing. I didn't know this existed.

I stayed for a while, and off I went to the next restaurant up the road. So I just did this little tour for the best part of a year. I learned some pretty basic stuff; like in Italy it's not just the same red sauce everywhere. It's all about regional cooking, very much like France. At the time, everyone in the U.S. was saying, "Oh, white sauces. That's northern Italian cuisine." That was the big buzz in those days. I was like, "What does that mean? So you put a little cream in your pasta, all right." So I learned there's really a dramatic difference between the regions. In Tuscany alone I saw the millions of ways in which they use bread. That was dramatic for me; it was a huge difference than what I saw growing up.

My grandmother was from Sicily. Her house always seemed to be full of the aroma of onions cooking in olive oil. That is still a scent that moves me deeply. I have fond memories of her making rabbit cacciatore. People were a little afraid of it because they thought we were cooking cat. My uncle, whom I was very close to, had a bakery in the Bronx but he was from Venice, and his true specialty was polenta. So Italian food wasn't foreign to me at all, but the culinary direction I went in was French. I attended The Culinary Institute of America and learned Escoffier and the mother sauces and all that. I think you need to study your foundation; it's important to understand where everything is coming from, and then you can expand your mind to other things. I used to get a lot of flack about turning mushroom caps. It was very hard for me to make these perfect ridges on the cap with a paring knife. I went down to the grocery store and I bought two flats of mushrooms and I sat in the herb room and I practiced until I finally figured it out. I learned something that day, and it was that for anything you learn, it takes discipline and dedication. Then you kind of tap into whatever talents you might have. But you need to push yourself to discover that talent.

After school, I worked under Jean-Jacques Rachou at La Côte Basque. Rick Moonen, Charlie Palmer, and David Bouley where all there, too. At one point Charlie and I were working side by side on the line. That's two big guys, and it didn't leave much room for anyone else.

At that time, Rachou was kind of on the edge. He was the one painting sauces on the plates and stuff. But he also made wonderful rustic dishes. No one makes a better cassoulet than Jean-Jacques. So when I chose to go to Italy, I wasn't rejecting French food. I knew that it could have a wonderful heartiness, too. But I was looking for more than recipes. I was looking, I realize now, for a relaxed and pleasurable way to eat.

That's what I would find in Italy. On our day off at the first place I worked at, everybody would get together and go somewhere to eat, and often we went to this place way up on a hillside. It was just this open space with canopies and tents scattered about. We sat at long tables, and everybody gathered around. There was a wood-burning oven, and there was a small kitchen. There were usually twelve or fif-

Chef's Story **Todd English**

111

teen of us at the table, and we drank the local wine and had unbeliev-able food. It was fun, it was family, and it was hours of enjoyment and celebrating life. I wouldn't say I had much of a business plan when I opened Olives, but I had a model.

Once I was back in the States, Michela Larson hired me to be the executive chef at her adventurous Italian project, Michela's, in Bos-ton. I was twenty-four, and it was all but overwhelming. There were no meatballs or bottles of chianti in straw baskets. Boston didn't know what gnocchi was, let alone risotto or tagliatelle. Though the work was gratifying, after four years of it I realized that if I was going to work that hard, I was going to work for myself.

I opened Olives in 1989. The economy was kind of in the doldrums, and everything was bad. But I finally raised the money, and I thought, "Okay, the economy stinks, but I've got to survive." I designed the whole kitchen. It was L-shaped. I have long arms, so I could reach the grill, the stove, and the wood-burning oven. I told myself if nobody came I could work this thing myself. I wanted it to be like the places I'd known in Italy. I wanted it to feel like a neighborhood place. I wanted my friends to be there, and to make new friends as well. I wanted it to be every-one's watering hole, and that's always been my thing. I just gravitated toward that approach without really putting that much thought into it. I just realized, this is who I am and this is what I love about food.

So we opened. We had five customers the first night, then by day three we went up to twenty, then a hundred, and then there were lines around the corner, and it never stopped. I remember my grandmother coming to the restaurant, and she was kind of, "Well, that's not really Italian cooking." And then my uncle came to my restaurant, and he saw polenta on like seventeen different things. I was on a polenta craze when I first came back, and we had butternut squash polenta, spinach polenta, raisin polenta, and all sorts of polenta. And he tells me, "Why do you have the polenta on the menu?" It was a generational difference. He might make polenta, but he didn't expect to see it on a

menu. They had known lean times; I'm drawn to cooking that starts from having less. I like the question "What do I do with this five-day-old bread?" because it can lead to great dishes. From my point of view, I've always looked to great peasant dishes and asked myself how I can modernize and elevate them.

I believe you should tell a story on every plate, and the story can be as simple as why those ingredients are together. Sometimes it's not about the prettiest food, but it's about just the flavors grabbing the palate. There needs to be a reason for everything to be on the plate. I disagree with the old-line French *entremetier* who would throw red peppers on the border of the plate just for color. But today we're in danger of doing exactly the same with micro greens. There should be a reason why everything that's on that plate is there. You see some menus today and you could take two dishes and switch the protein between them and it wouldn't make any difference—where's the inspiration there?

Today's cooking is ingredient driven. In the old days, a chef could do things that the average customer was never going to try at home. Customers now get their vegetables at the Farmers Market, too. As a chef, you have to ask yourself, why are you paying me to slice that tomato and put olive oil and salt on it? Our challenge is how do we grace the ingredients and elevate them? Maybe we take that same tomato with salt and olive oil and add a squeeze of fresh horseradish or brush the tomato with very light basil cream. That begins the layering of flavors; that's the magic that can occur between cutting board, oven, and plate.

I started down the road of expanding my business when I opened an Olives in Las Vegas. With that restaurant we went from fifty seats to a hundred and eighty seats. That's from maybe a hundred and forty dinners in a night to six hundred a night. It was scary. I'm not sure without Steve Wynn and Elizabeth Blau, of the Bellagio, I would ever have done it. They came to Boston a few times, and I went out there. But even after being wined and dined, I said, "I don't think I can do this. It's not me." It's a whole different culture. Their focus is for it to be part of the hotel; I'm a hundred percent about the restaurant, and the guests that come into the restaurant. Steve Wynn really taught me that I wasn't giving up something; I was doing it in a bigger way. We got all the managerial support that we needed, and that provided a broader base to grow from, and we did.

The day actually comes when you feel confident about expansion. Then we got contacted by the St. Regis in Aspen and Starwood Hotels, because they were excited about what was going on in Vegas, and so it sort of steamrolled. Eventually I had the opportunity to open in New York, which I've always wanted to do. Hotels have big infrastructures that make it possible. What I do is go in with my expertise and that of the chefs who have worked for me for years, and I go in and make sure that the chicken's cooked right and that the food's getting out to the tables on time, and that we're creating, to the best of our abilities, that little intangible excitement that restaurants bring.

I was one of the early ones to start expanding, and I got a lot of criticism. The press argued that because I wasn't always in the kitchen it couldn't be my food. That's hard to hear, and you sort of lose face. Now people understand that things have changed. The modern restaurateur stands for something—it's a signature, it's a brand, it's a stamp, it's a seal. The nature of the restaurant has changed, too. It's the modern living room, in a sense. People work hard, they play hard, and often they don't really have the time to gather at everyone's home. So they go to these places, these lounges, these living rooms, these restaurants, to celebrate life. I think that's really why I like it. It's about having fun, not at all taking away from the food and the quality and the preparation and the amount of work that goes into it, but it's just more about the actual experience. That always has been my thing. I want you to have a good time. I want you to have fun. I want you to roll up your sleeves, and that's all I care about.

I opened Olives with that really great sort of naïve love of what I was doing. I had a passion for nurturing food that I wanted to share. Then all of a sudden I had people yelling at the front door when I'd try to close. I'd be, "Look, it's eleven thirty. I'm not cooking anymore. I'm done. Come back tomorrow." And they'd shout back, "I've been waiting three and a half hours." So there is a loss there. You lose some innocence as the years pass. Those are days that aren't coming back. I always thought at some point the job would get easier. But it never stops. It's a tough lifestyle. You're on every night. You're working long hours. But the other side of it is, if you truly love the business, you eat, live, breathe, and sleep it. It's a business that is constantly pushing you to discover talents you never thought you had. You know what it takes from you, but you also know what it gives.

Dean Fearing

Dean Fearing has been called the father of Southwestern cuisine, drawing his influence from backyard barbecues while growing up in eastern Kentucky. He is executive chef at Fearing's at the Ritz-Carlton Hotel in Dallas, and has an extensive gourmet food line. He has received the James Beard Foundation Award for Best Chef, Southwest, graced the cover of *Gourmet* magazine, and cooked on every national morning television show. He also has an all-chef band, The Barbwires.

I grew up in Ashland, in eastern Kentucky, on the Ohio River, where Ohio, Kentucky, and West Virginia meet. It was a steel mill town. My father had worked in the local small-town department store, then become manager of the town's "fine" hotel, the Henry Clay. I was lucky enough to have two grandmothers living nearby. Both were fine cooks, and I was raised on unbelievable meals. The holidays were a rotating series of spreads, when we'd go from one house to the other. My mother's mother in particular was a fine country cook. What was canned she and my grandfather had canned; what was pickled they had pickled. That way, in all seasons, we had bounty from their garden, whether it was canned beans or corn, pickled beets and cantaloupes, or blueberry conserves. Our relatives would bring us seeds for tomatoes in paper bags. No one applied the word *heirloom* to vegetables in those days, but these were the real thing; each generation passed the seeds of their best plants on to the next.

Often on a Saturday night we'd get in the car and drive the thirteen miles to Huntington, West Virginia, and go to a place called Bailey's Cafeteria. I always had the chicken-fried steak with real milk gravy. That's gravy where after you've cooked the chicken you put a little milk into the pan to thicken up with whatever browned crumbs are still stuck to the bottom, and maybe thicken it up with some of the flour from the breading. Seasoning was strictly salt and pepper. No one in my family knew what a jalapeño pepper was. My grandparents might have put a little spicy something in their pickled vegetables, but chile-derived heat never went any further than that.

In 1965 my father joined Holiday Inn, and we started to travel throughout the Midwest. Saint Louis, Milwaukee, Akron, Richmond, Indiana—I lived in them all. Holiday Inn really put hotels like the Henry Clay out of business. They all had a pool and an atmosphere that at the time was considered cutting edge. They also had restaurants which, while not fine, were usually better than most found in small towns. By the time we were teenagers, my brother and I had to report to the hotel after school, and whoever didn't show up for work at the second shift, my brother and I would have to work it. Maintenance, laundry, cooking—we did it all. We hated it until payday; then we loved it.

What we really wanted to do was be musicians. I played guitar all through high school and during my short-lived college career. I went to Ball State, quit after a year, and joined my brother in Columbia, Missouri, playing in garage bands and cooking wherever I could to pay the bills. My dad wanted to open a restaurant in the historical part of Louisville, a project that would have required much restoration, and I joined him there to help with the process. But the government grants for that fell through, and soon I was back to cooking at the Holiday Inn, and a paycheck wouldn't make up for all the fun places I felt I'd left behind.

It was time to make a decision about the direction of my life. I can still remember the moment when my dad called me into his office at the Holiday Inn in Louisville. I think he'd steeled himself as much for this conversation as I had. In his mind things had gone on long enough. The hair, the clothes, the hippie attitude, the guitar noise coming from the garage—those might pass. But dreams of being a rock star—somebody had to talk sense into the boy. He had seen an article in the *Courier-Journal* about a chef who had come to town and who planned on giving classes, he said. He thought I might be interested in going down to talk to him.

"But I want to be in a rock band," I said, knowing that sentence alone was enough to make my father wince. "I'm asking for five minutes of your time," he answered. "If you don't like it, you can leave. Just go down and shake his hand."

I got in my '66 red fastback VW I'd picked up in Newton, Iowa, for eight hundred dollars (earned during all those random hotel shifts) and drove to the Jefferson Community College, in downtown Louisville. At least afterward he couldn't say I hadn't tried.

The man I met there might as well have been Basil Rathbone. He had a thin mustache, he spoke with an English accent, and he wore his toque cocked at an angle that certainly didn't suggest he was a seventy-two-year-old retired chef. What he was doing in the Jefferson

119

Community College of Louisville, Kentucky, would have seemed like a mystery to most. The answer was that while corporate chef for Hilton in Hawaii, he had fallen in love and married a woman half his age and had followed her to her hometown when she returned.

He sat me down and asked me a bit about my experience. I told him a bit about it. He seemed politely interested, and finally interrupted me to ask if I'd ever braised anything. *Braise*. The word kind of hung in the air between us. It sounded wonderful, and amazingly it didn't involve a Fender guitar. "No, I have not, sir," I answered. He nodded. "Sauté?" This word sounded dramatic. I could not say I had ever sautéed anything, either. At that stage he excused himself from the small office, and I got up to look at the certificate on the wall. It was a diploma of an apprenticeship at the Ritz Hotel in London, signed by Auguste Escoffier. When he walked back in, I understood that for the first time in my life I was seeing a real chef.

Harvey Colgin was his name, and for the next few years he would be the most important influence on my life. We were cooking for the student body, and we'd get there about six thirty a.m. and start our prep. Harvey would regale us with stories of the old days at the Ritz, when a cook might kick an apprentice into an oven he was lighting. Cooks stole each other's prep, and a junior chef might walk over to an unfortunate youngster to tell them their cut was not up to standard and throw it all away. But through it all there was always this push for all of us to learn and expand what we knew. Because I was so interested, I was the one on whom this encouragement was focused the most. I was still working nights at the Holiday Inn, and when I told him I needed recipes, he volunteered them, often writing them in the most elegant handwriting I had ever seen. Finally, he said I should go further than he himself could

provide in the community college setting. He got me into The Culinary Institute of America in 1976, and away I went.

My first job out of school was in La Maisonette in Cincinnati, under George Haidon, a fantastic chef who was the first to import fresh fish from France overnight. We'd be in Cincinnati working with the most beautiful turbot and those perfect little rouget with their vermilion scales that you get in Provence. In 1980, I was executive sous-chef at The Mansion on Turtle Creek, leaving to open Agnew's in 1982. We were the only white-tablecloth American restaurant in Dallas at the time.

By then, I was already working on an idea: how to remain elegant and defy the expectations of the times by not serving dishes such as Dover sole with brown butter. It's an idea that many of us were coming at from our different perspectives. Perhaps because I'm not a native Texan, the question was very clear. How could Texas's strong sense of identity stop dead cold when it came to elegant food?

That would be the question my career would eventually revolve around when I returned to The Mansion as chef in 1984, and today at Fearing's at the Ritz-Carlton.

It wasn't without challenging moments. I think young chefs today might not actually understand what it is like to have to fight your way out of the bag of expectations. When I came up with our lobster taco with yellow tomato salsa, I went out to the dining room to explain it to the waiters' meeting that was held every night at five thirty. They gathered around, and I said, "Okay, the special tonight is a lobster taco with a homemade flour tortilla wrapped in spinach with jalapeño jack on a salsa made with yellow tomatoes." All of a sudden from the background I hear, "Oh my God, you have to be kidding me," and it's the Italian maître d'. He said, "Are you crazy. They can buy this at the Tex-Mex place down the street." I said, "Look, Jean-Pierre, roll with it for tonight and we'll see what happens." By seven thirty, we were out. Jean-Pierre rushed in to the kitchen. "What do you mean you're out? They love it. Make more, make more!"

Southwestern food achieved several things. It allowed heat to come into the spectrum of sensations that were allowed; it gave indigenous products a new context—that of the elegant restaurant—in which to refresh and delight; and, very important, it gave our many cooks of Mexican ancestry the true pleasure that they didn't have to drop their identities at the kitchen door. I would be running flavors by them, asking for their input on a sauce or a salad. Because our produce company didn't carry cilantro, they were the ones who brought it to work. That kind of atmosphere makes a huge difference in a kitchen, because there is suddenly a connection between the cooks and the menu. I frankly think it makes a restaurant feel alive.

For us chefs who came at the idea together, it formed friendships that we'll have for the rest of our lives. Southwestern was promotable; however oversimplified it was, the idea that these renegade cooks were firing up the chiles had a certain charm.

My friendship with Robert Del Grande came just out of precisely the sort of gathering that we would often find ourselves at. I was talking to his wife, Mimi, who's great at getting to know people. "So what do you like to do other than cook?" she asked. "Play guitar," I said. "Robert plays guitar, too." I saw Robert across the room and I ran over to him. "Man, what kind of guitar do you have?" He said, "A Martin D35." I said, "I have a Martin D18." It wasn't long before promotional tours turned into concerts in hotel rooms that were so much fun even the room service waiters didn't want to leave.

Being a cook is a hard profession; there are moments of struggle and moments of self-doubt. You are constantly trying to communicate who you are through flavors, without being obvious about it, with nuance and finesse. For me, smoking is one of the ways I've always done it. It introduces a note that captivates people. I can achieve it as simply as cold-smoking onions over cherry wood that I'll purée into a Caesar salad dressing. That smoky taste for me evokes Kentucky and the country around Ashland that my family is from. Sometimes I can even see what Harvey Colgin saw in me. It's what every chef sees when an enthusiastic young person works in their kitchen: a person to whom you can pass on what you know and who will use that to forge their own path. Harvey lived until he was ninety-eight, and I was in touch with him to the end. I still think he left me alone with his diploma on purpose, just so that he could reel me in.

Bobby Flay

A graduate of The French Culinary Institute, Bobby Flay was mentored by Jonathan Waxman and Wolfgang Puck, and brought the Southwest to New York with his first restaurant, Mesa Grill. Bolo and Bar Americain followed. He also has restaurants in Las Vegas and Atlantic City. He has hosted a variety of shows on the Food Network, including *BBQ with Bobby Flay*, *Boy Meets Grill*, and *Hot Off the Grill with Bobby Flay*. As master instructor of The French Culinary Institute, Bobby Flay is educating the next generation of chefs.

You can't hang out in my kitchen. I won't fire you; you'll just leave because everybody else around you will make you feel uncomfortable naturally, because everybody else works hard and gets along. We like a nice environment. We like to have fun while we're cooking, but there's no hanging out. There never was.

Cooking allowed me to do something else other than just sit around with my friends. I was eighteen when I walked into Joe Allen's kitchen in the Theater District of Manhattan. I had just graduated from high school. I was dressed in a pair of jeans and sneakers and a sweatshirt and I didn't really know what to expect. I was making salad dressings, washing lettuces, chopping vegetables. I didn't realize I was going to be a chef. I was happy to just have a job. But it also made me feel that I had an interest in something, because before that I'd just been a high school kid who hated going to high school. My mom and dad gave me perfect direction and gave me anything I needed to succeed in school, and I just said, "I don't think so."

In kitchens, I found a place that gave me something else to think about, so that for the first time ever I could envision a future. I remember the day when I woke up and looked up at the ceiling and said, "This is something I really want to go and do." And that was a big turning point for me, because it gave me focus. It was about six months after I'd started, and a series of small victories had led up to it. Okay, now I'm working the sauté station and I can do busy services. And I can feed a lot of people. Or I can do five omelets at a time. These were small victories, but each gave me the sense of "I can do it."

One day Joe Allen came down into the kitchen and he said, "You know there's this new school opening up. You should check it out." It was The French Culinary Institute. Even though my cooking isn't French, learning from the chefs at the FCI gave me structure and discipline and the understanding of how cooking works. The first food I got into was Southwestern. I worked for Jonathan Waxman for about three years at Jams and Bud's and this place called Hulot's. There was all this blue corn and fresh and dried chili peppers all over the kitchen, and I fell in love with the ingredients.

So now, here I am, this New York City kid, and I wanted to go to the source. I got on a plane and worked in a bunch of kitchens around the Southwest, in Texas and New Mexico. I worked with Robert Del Grande and Dean Fearing and Stephan Pyles and Mark Kiffin and Kevin Rathbun, and I have to say Texas has been a very special state for me. There's no prouder place. I love the food, and my wife comes from there.

Mesa Grill opened first, and I think it gave me my signature flavor profile. What do I cook? Before you get into anything else, it's important to remember how important salt and pepper is. Particularly, salt, which brings out all the other flavors and gets them together. Without salt, all the flavors that you put into a dish remain separate for some reason. Don't ask me why. I'm not a scientist. It's one of those things, like glue for other ingredients. You have to keep one ingredient as the main one, and so must balance the flavors.

When I use a lot of ingredients that have spicy and pungent flavors, I'll balance that out with things that are sweet, like honey or maple syrup, so they don't overpower a piece of chicken or fish. I never make food that's burn-your-mouth-out spicy. What I say is we employ chile peppers for accent not injury.

There's a dish that's been on the menu since the first day. It's shrimp and roasted garlic tamale, and to me it says, "Mesa Grill." You know, it's got the classic southwest vehicle, which is tamale. We make ours with fresh corn, and we don't use lard; we use lots of butter, but then we get some really great gulf shrimp and add garlic and cilantro. We make a sauce out of it. I mean, you shouldn't have to spell it out, in my opinion. If you've eaten around, and I put that dish in front of you, you would say, "This is something that Mesa Grill would serve," and that's important.

We opened Bolo three years later, and that answered the second important question: Who am I cooking for? At the time it opened, the only Spanish restaurants in New York were sort of red-and-white-tablecloth restaurants that served cheap sangria and overcooked paella. I loved them, they were fun restaurants, but they didn't take the food

too seriously. I thought good Spanish food was underrepresented. So we found a location by happenstance, and I said to my partners, "I love this space. I want to open a Spanish restaurant." They're like, "Why? Why a Spanish restaurant?" So I knew it was going to be a challenge to serve what I thought of as Spanish food in New York. First of all I'd have to deal with critics who were also going to say, "Why? You're from Seventy-eighth and Third Avenue. What do you know about paella?" And that's actually a fair question, but I don't open restaurants that are traditional or authentic to a T. It's not what I really know how to do. I don't have that sort of background. I can love the energy of Barcelona, but what I try to do is open restaurants for New Yorkers. From a business and a cooking standpoint, that's the only thing I know how to do. So as far as Bolo is concerned, I'm just borrowing the flavors of Spain. I hope that's okay with Spain.

I have three restaurants in New York now, and at some stage I figured, "Gee, I'd better try and have some kind of a schedule." I do have a schedule, but in this business that rarely works out. Not for me anyway. In this business things happen that you don't expect every single day, basically every single hour, whether it's personnel or a customer or bathroom floods. I'm very lucky to have the partners I do. I never once looked at a financial statement of my company. I know that every nickel is going exactly where it has to go. My responsibility is the kitchens and keeping up the flavors. Mesa and Bolo and Bar Americain are very different, but all the food is very well flavored. I walk around my kitchens tasting the food and I know right away if somebody is taking shortcuts, because the food just doesn't pop. You've got to taste everything. I think there are too many cooks who cook and don't taste. I always say if you're not chewing in my kitchen, you're not cooking.

But I also want to inspire the cooks. I think the greatest thing I can give my chefs is to let them do their job. I don't micromanage them. We're on top of them and we want them to be better cooks and we want them to better themselves within the company, but it's not obsessive. I also try and make sure that for the employees it's not just a job. If you can actually inspire people in different ways, besides the obvious, that's a good thing. I send my sous-chefs at Bolo to Spain so that they become inspired, or send them to the Aspen Food & Wine Festival. This gives them something to look forward to that will enhance them, not just for me to get something out of it. It's more about them thinking, "This is really a great place to work, and Bobby's thinking of me besides, 'Can he cook the steak right?'"

A lot of people think I spend all of my time doing TV. Actually, I don't. The great thing about cable is that you shoot it a little, and they show it a lot. So that's really helpful to me because I can shoot thirteen shows and they can run for years. Basically I split my time; eighty percent of it I'm in our restaurants and twenty percent on TV.

When I started with the Food Network it was a lot different than it is now. They had zero dollars and they were in some shabby studio on the West Side. Basically the only chefs they were having as guests were chefs that could take a taxi. So if you weren't in Manhattan, you weren't going on the Food Network. Like all things, they started to grow and become more successful, and they offered me a show called *Grilling in Hawaii*. I named the show *Grillin' 'n Chillin'*, but they definitely wanted grilling. They said, "You know that guy Jack McDavid, that's a friend of yours? Can you call over and ask him if he'd like to do a show with you?" And I said, "Sure, I'll call him." That was really the way it happened.

So Jack and I went to Hawaii and shot forty-two half-hour shows in six days. No script. They would kind of throw the food on the table and say, "All right. Turn the cameras on. Let's go." And I get more questions about that show than any other show I've done. People ask, "What happened to that show? I loved that show. Where's that guy? Where's Jack?"

The funny thing is that the inspiration often comes from TV. I did a show called *Food Nation,* which was really the most rewarding show for me from a chef's standpoint, but I didn't cook; I learned. I traveled the whole country eating great food, learning about the nation through food. And that's basically how Bar Americain was born. I also became a Bourbon drinker because I went to Lexington, Kentucky, for the show.

Iron Chef is different because it is competitive. I don't really think of that as a television show for me. I have to stand on the podium and fold my arms, and I have dry ice blowing out around my head. However, and I mean this with all sincerity, when I get to the kitchen at *Iron Chef,* it's an athletic event. I'm highly competitive. I don't want to lose. I want to cook great food, and you have sixty minutes to cook with an ingredient that you didn't know about five minutes ago. It's very, very hard to do, but it's exhilarating for me, because my athletic career is over, so this is sort of my athletic outlet, and it's very challenging. Listen, every chef that comes into the kitchen against me has been gunning for me in their heads for three months, because they know ahead of time they're going to do it.

I did *Iron Chef Japan* and I went over to Tokyo. If you've seen the movie *Lost in Translation,* that was basically my life. I stayed in that hotel. I had to meet a lot of people. They were shoving me in vans, taking me to photo shoots. They really want to know "Do you think you can win?" "What happens if it's lobster?" They really get you thinking about it and get you to buy into what's happening. You're so competitive by the time you get there that it's almost like a thoroughbred racehorse when it first gets to the track. They know they're supposed to run.

I did not go to college and I didn't take any business courses or anything along those lines. I learned from life and from watching people—the people who do it right. I watch them very closely, and I'm not ashamed to say that. I like to mimic those things, taking small things that make them successful, and use them as part of my own program. When people ask which chefs I idolize, Wolfgang Puck is at the top of my list. He helped people like me have a career. He helped culinary schools. He had a vision, and maybe it was just luck, but I doubt it because he is a smart man. He saw there was an opportunity to serve great food that wasn't just French—food that was whimsical and that could be great. There were other cuisines. He could put smoked salmon on a pizza and people could be wowed by it, not just by the idea but also by the taste and the concept. He was also the first chef to understand the importance of Las Vegas. For a long time I didn't want to go there. My daughter had just been born, and I wasn't

131

going to take on that lifestyle, which means getting on a plane a few times a month and going there, and then a couple of years ago Caesars Palace called and said, "Why aren't you here?" And I explained to them why, and they said, "Well, we're going to make you come to Vegas. We'd like to sit down and talk to you about this."

I think the biggest challenge was melding the philosophies. A casino is a corporate environment, and at our restaurants we have a sort of independent style, so the big question was, could we fit into a corporate structure and remain independent within it? It's worked out great, even though it required a lot of balancing of personnel. I moved seven of my chefs there, and they absolutely love it. From a lifestyle point of view, one of the guys grew up in Brooklyn, could barely afford a one-bedroom there his whole life. He moved to Vegas, and now he's got three bedrooms and a pool. He's happy living like a king, and he loves his job. So we treat it like a real one of our restaurants, not an outpost, which, I think, is sometimes easy to do if you're not there all the time. I can't live that life of just putting my name on it. I can't go to sleep knowing you're going to go to Vegas and go to a Bobby Flay restaurant and not have Bobby Flay food.

The great thing about the Food Network is that a lot of kids watch it. I mean, you'd be amazed how many children watch the Food Network. In my daughter Sophie's class—she's in fourth grade—the whole class watches it. (But Sophie has no interest in it; she watches the Disney Channel.) These kids are unbelievable, at ten years old. I told her we were going down to a food festival in Miami and there were actually kids' cooking classes, so I was taking her with me. I said, "Hey, if you want to, I'll get you into one of these kids' cooking classes." And she says, "Dad, cooking was your dream." It's like she feels, "All right, the cooking part, we have that covered in the family. I'm going to rescue animals or something."

I don't want to open thirty-five restaurants. I don't want to have five Bar Americains and seven Mesa Grills. I can't imagine over the next two or three years trying to open restaurants. It's too hard, and at some point you lose the quality. I still feel that we're on top of our game, and I like being there. When I opened Mesa Grill, I was twenty-five years old and not quite broken. I had a lot going on at a very young age, and so I think what happened was that I didn't really sort of stop for long enough to understand that what you say can affect people, whether they're standing next to you or across the country. I think as I got a little bit more mature I sort of mellowed. The fact is that it's a lot more satisfying to be nicer to people and to guide people and to stop and hear everybody's story who wants to tell it.

I like hip-hop and reggae; I like music that has a lot of soul. Sometimes when I'm listening to reggae I think of jerk seasonings and mango chutneys. I tend to look at things through food. I also love playing golf and dancing with my wife. I've been taking the subway my whole life, and if people say to me, "I can't believe you're on the subway," I respond that I wouldn't think of going any other way. First of all, it's better, given the traffic on the street, but I just don't want to lose who I am. I get up and go to work, whether it's to my office or to one of the restaurants or to go shoot a television show. It's a job, and I think that as soon as I start feeling like I'm a TV star, it's going to be a bad day.

For me, cooking has been everything. It really has given me a sense of belonging. Among my peers I would like to be known as somebody who is true to my profession, somebody who is a hard worker and who is known for a certain style of cuisine. That would be plenty for me.

Suzanne
Goin

A native of Los Angeles, Suzanne Goin has traveled the world honing her skills. She spent time in Europe at French restaurants, including L'Arpège; Pain, Adour et Fantasie; and Pâtisserie Christian Pottier. Upon returning to the United States, Goin worked at Chez Panisse, was hired by Todd English as sous-chef at Olives in Boston, and later became the chef at Alloro. Goin returned to Los Angeles to work at Campanile and later opened her own restaurants, Lucques, named after her favorite French olive; A.O.C., which specializes in cheeses and other small plates; and The Hungry Cat. *Food & Wine* magazine has named her Best New Chef.

I think that when you can say that Mary Ann Mobley was your Brownie leader you can qualify as an L.A. girl. After all, not every Brownie leader has credits that stretch from movies with Elvis to *Falcon Crest*. Unfortunately I wasn't the most perfect Brownie. We all had to have flower names, and I started calling everybody names like Dirt and Weed. I had a little streak of smart-aleck in me. I'm not sure why I was like that at school because when our parents would take my sister and me to restaurants, we were very well behaved. Seeing this world that had two sides was really fascinating, and gradually drew me in. At Perino's, we split the cannelloni, at L'Hermitage we were fussed over, precisely because we were well-behaved children, and when we made it to Moulin de Mougins and my father ordered a *loup de mer* that came with perfect scales of cucumber, I was completely entranced.

My parents were both serious foodies. They never ordered the kiddie meal or the plate of pasta with butter for the children. Most Friday evenings there was some pretty serious discussions about where we would eat Saturday night, Sunday lunch and dinner. If that was to be at home, we went about planning the menus.

It seemed only natural when, as a seventeen-year-old at school, we were given two weeks to learn something we'd always wanted to learn and I chose cooking. I went to the back door of Ma Maison, one of my parents' favorite places, and Patrick Terrail, the owner, came out to speak with me. He was very kind, but he essentially looked at me as only someone who is running a very busy restaurant would look at a seventeen-year-old who comes asking for training.

Two weeks later, when I showed up on the appointed date, he had forgotten all about it, and he kind of led me into the kitchen and introduced me to the chef, and that was it. I had expected that I would be following someone and taking notes, but Wolfgang had just left to open Spago and they were short-staffed, and with a modicum of training they put me to work—which I far preferred. The pastry chef showed me how to make a raspberry sorbet; then I had to make a strawberry one. She showed me one little fruit tart, and I had to make five. It was an incredible feeling during service to see one scoop of that sorbet or one of those tarts get carried out on a plate by a waiter to a paying guest. I had made it, I felt, to the other side.

But much was to happen before I finally would get there. I studied history and international relations at Brown. My dad used to say that I put into the computer "Farthest from home, hardest to get to, and most expensive," and Brown came up. That's because I didn't succumb to all the bribes with which he tried to entice me to go to UCLA. My mother's family was from Connecticut, so I had spent time there and I was looking forward to the whole East Coast college experience.

In my final year, I wrote a thesis on the first American diplomats to study the Soviet Union. It was actually fascinating because at the Library of Congress there were all these documents that no one had ever opened before, and I got to compare what these diplomats had reported back and what the State Department had summarized. There were huge differences.

While at Brown I hadn't given up on restaurants at all. On the contrary, my fascination with them had only grown stronger. I had gotten a job as a waitress at Al Forno, this dreamy little restaurant on Steeple Street in Providence. They asked me if I had any experience, and I crossed my fingers and said I did. I worked almost a year as a waitress before a position opened up in the kitchen to do salads and desserts and help George and Johanne, the owners. It was a great place to learn, because their aesthetic sense of simplicity and perfection was so defined. We would slice the prosciutto for the antipasto and make all the desserts to order. These things were happening at the same time all through the night. If you wanted an apple tart you ordered it at the beginning of your meal, and then we had to slice the apples on the slicer that the prosciutto was on, so in the middle of the service you're cleaning the slicer and making tarts.

Jaime D'Oliveira, who had been the chef at Al Forno, was open-

ing up his own place, called Angels, and I went to work for him for a year. By then I sort of knew that I was going to be in this business and that I hoped to have my own place, and I thought it would be a really good experience to be at a restaurant from the start. But that was a crucial moment in another respect. I had just graduated college and I had to make a decision about my future. Was I going to grad school or to cook? I knew what it was going to be. I had to call my parents, and they'd just spent twelve trillion dollars on college, and I said, "I'm going to work in a restaurant at eight dollars an hour." In my recollection they were fine with it. But my sister remembers it differently. "Don't you remember that you and Dad didn't talk to each other for two months?" I may have blocked that out. I do remember, though, that once I got a job at Chez Panisse, a restaurant my father loved, he finally knew that it was going to be okay.

I got that job by writing a letter at three in the morning. I'd reached a stage where I wanted some guidance, a mentor, I'm not sure what. But I'd done my year in Angels, and I wasn't sure whether to move back to L.A. or what to do, and I just wrote this letter asking if I could come and talk to someone. After writing the letter I went out and mailed it in the middle of the night because I knew if the letter was still there in the morning I would lose my nerve. About a week later I got a call from Alice Waters's office, and they said, "When you're out here, why don't you give us a call and come in and talk to someone."

I did that. And the person I talked to was Catherine Brandel, the chef of the café upstairs, and I was just supposed to come and meet her, and afterward she said, "Well, do you want to hang out tonight?" I said, "Oh, yeah." So I stayed through service, and then she said, "Well, do you want to come back tomorrow?" And I said of course I did. And after two or three days there, she asked me, "Would you ever consider working here?" I said, "Well, yeah, I never thought that was an option."

So I ended up coming back for a tryout, where I had to make lunch for ten people, Alice herself and the chef Paul Bertolli among them. It was the end of October and I had planned this whole ode-to-fall menu, but the Bay Area was having an Indian summer and it was ninety-five degrees on the day of the lunch. I had to redo the entire menu, which I think was good, because it made me much looser. About five minutes before the meal, the waiter—Jonathan I would later learn—came over and asked me what wines I'd chosen. Wines! He helped me choose the wines, and after the meal, when I went out to talk to them, my wine selection was the first thing they praised. They asked a little about my career. And I said I'd learned a lot from books. What books? Right then my mind went blank. The names of Paula Wolfert and Richard Olney and Elizabeth David just wouldn't come. I thought they'd think I was faking it, but they understood a person can be nervous in such a situation, and eventually they offered me the job: pasta-lettuce girl at Chez Panisse.

I don't want to give myself as an example of someone who did everything right, but I do understand that moving forward in this profession has to do with how you approach the act of learning. I get lots of letters from people who are thinking of a career change and I try to answer them. People took time for me. I always say the same thing: the first thing you need to do is find a restaurant where you can work for free for a week and see what it's really like, because it's not what you think it is. That's the first group. The second group is those who are already in the kitchen. I get very frustrated when a young cook says something like, "I just feel I should be learning more." Okay, well, this entire restaurant is sitting here. Just working your station may not be fully taking advantage of what it offers. If you came in an hour early and worked with the prep guy, or on your day off and hung out with the grill cook, you would learn more. There are people who just want to be spoonfed. "Teach me, teach me." It's like, "No, learn."

That is what I would spend the next several years doing. Catherine Brandel helped me go to France, and I worked for Didier Oudill, down in the Landes, and I even got into Arpège, in Paris, doing my infamous door-knocking, showing-up routine. I then went to Boston and I worked at Olives, where I was Todd's sous-chef. It was a great kitchen—very high energy, very passionate about food, and with Pearl Jam blasting at arena volume.

In some ways Todd and I are very similar and in some ways we're very different. He's the more-more guy, and I'm the less-less girl. We would have these menu meetings and we would be in the office late at night going over ideas, and I'd come in and I'd say, "I have these five ideas of things we could do," and Todd would say, "Great," and he'd turn it all into one dish.

But being sous-chef and being chef are two very different things. When you're sous-chef you can take the glory when the glory comes, but when things are not so good then it's all on the chef. The whole thing is your idea, and if people don't like it, it's you. I was finally ready to take that stage, and Todd actually helped me get my first chef position, at a small place called Alloro, in Boston's North End. Though the neighborhood is Italian, the owner was Portuguese. When I first started, I said, "Just so you know, I don't have that much Italian experience." He brushed that off. "Oh, that's fine. Just make whatever you want and we'll give it an Italian name." So he named every dish. I made salmon with red wine butter; he'd say, "Oh, good. Salmone." He was very supportive, and he never said I couldn't put a dish on the menu. In fact, he was the person who first turned me on to Portuguese flavors, which today I love.

I always knew I wanted to come back to L.A. Unfortunately I came back because my dad was ill. I got to spend four months with him before he passed away. My mom really needed me, and it was nice to be with my sister. Basically, after my dad died, my mom and I sat in the TV room with the shades down and watched *Friends* and drank red wine every night. Finally I said, "Mom, I need to go get a job or I'm going to kill myself." Even though I was from L.A., I hadn't cooked there since a little job I'd had at L'Orangerie, when I was nineteen. I met Octavio Becerra, from Patina, and he helped me get into Pinot Bistro. I worked for Fred Eric, too, and eventually I got to Campanile, and I said to Mark Peel I could commit to three months. He said, "Bet you we can get you to stay for six." Eventually I stayed two years, and Mark placed great trust in me. I rose to *chef de cuisine,* and I had to learn things that were new to me, such as finances and schedules and inventory. This was great because by then I knew I wanted to open my own place soon.

I had met Caroline Styne through a friend who had been saying for ages we should meet because she was the manager of a place called Jones, in Hollywood. People often say, "You should meet so-and-so and you'll get along great," and it's not always the case. But with Caroline, it was. Pretty soon we were going around to restaurants and we'd say, "What do you think of this glass? What about the tablecloth?" We started feeling each other out, and soon we were looking for spaces together. Since I'd already started the process, I had an attorney and I told him I wanted to go into business with Caroline. "Do you know anything about this woman?" he asked me. "Well, she has really good taste," I said, "and I like her." "Have you worked with her before?" "No." It's the kind of conversation that can make a lawyer nervous.

Eventually we found the space where Lucques would be located, and we scraped together the money, borrowing from friends and family. We raised $450,000, and we got a line of credit for the last $100,000, which my mom co-signed, since I was living in an apartment. Some of the other backers were old neighbors of ours, and I said to my mother, "At least if you lose the house, you were going to have to leave the neighborhood anyway." Though I'd had the opportunity to learn a bit about finances as chef at Campanile, I still had a lot to learn. A chef had once told me, "Never sign a personal guarantee." After we got our liquor license, we went to see Southern Wine and Spirits about setting up an account. At the end of the conversation, they said, "Okay, here's the personal guarantee." I said, "Oh, I don't sign those." The man said, "Well, then you're not going to have any liquor." After we signed the first one, Caroline and I had to go out for martinis because we were so freaked out. We kind of looked at each other and said, "Well, if this doesn't work out, we're really screwed."

Thankfully it has worked. We not only have Lucques but a small-plates place called A.O.C., nearby on Third Street, and my husband, David, and I have The Hungry Cat, which is a small fish-focused place in Hollywood. We are very appreciative of the popularity of the restaurants, but we're also conscious to keep their individuality. We try to follow our hearts and passions, and open places we would like to go to. For me a great part of being a chef is responding to the particular and unique things in life. Beautiful arugula, for example, just makes me happy. When it has texture and bite and pepper and crunch, I just feel like the farm has come into the kitchen and it's a reinforcement of why food means what it means to me. It allows me to layer flavors on top of it—perhaps dates, a bit of blood orange, an almond, and a sliver of a dry cheese—and its sharpness keeps the flavors from being muddied and the total effect is crisp and clean.

In *Simple French Food*, Richard Olney writes, "the flavors of Provencal food tend to be direct and uncomplicated, reflecting the sharp clarity of the light and the landscape." As a native of Los Angeles, I am very aware of that special clear light we can get in fall and winter. I think that something as simple as the quality of light can have an effect on the way one perceives the world and tries to communicate it through cooking. What makes you a chef is mysterious. Lots of things come into it. I learned great and essential Mediterranean food in a kitchen where Pearl Jam was blasting. I learned about Portuguese food in an Italian restaurant in Boston's North End. I think the mix itself is the thing. You're constantly depositing information in your mind until it fuses with your personality. You knock on lots of doors trying to get in, and at some stage you stop knocking and it's what's inside you that speaks.

Thomas **Keller**

Thomas Keller learned to cook while working at the Palm Beach restaurant that his mother managed. He moved to France, where he worked at restaurants such as Taillevent, Guy Savoy, and Le Pré Catelan. He eventually moved to California, where he started his restaurants The French Laundry, Bouchon, and Bouchon Bakery, all in Yountville, California. He has also opened restaurants in Las Vegas and New York, including Per Se, given four stars by the *New York Times*. Per Se also received three Michelin stars, making Keller the only American-born chef to receive this honor. Keller was named America's Best Chef by *Time* magazine and has received seven awards from the James Beard Foundation.

My mother ran a restaurant in Florida called the Palm Beach Yacht Club. It was a lunch place, very small, forty seats. It sat at the end of a dock, and businessmen from West Palm Beach would come there and have lunch. There were two purveyors: one brought everything the restaurant could need, from meat to cleaning chemicals; the other brought the bread. In the summer after I graduated from high school, my best friend and I ran the restaurant. I hired him as my comrade, my cook, and my sous-chef. Neither one of us had ever cooked. We ordered all the food, we maintained the restaurant, and we cleaned the kitchen. It was our club. That was the summer of 1974. I was eighteen.

My biggest challenge every day was making the hollandaise for the eggs Benedict. My brother Joseph taught me how to make it, how to whisk the six yolks to the proper consistency and temperature, where they would emulsify with the clarified butter. The process fascinated me. Unlike the mix of paprika, lemon juice, and store-bought mayonnaise that we used to dab on the lobster tails before placing them in the broiler, making a hollandaise involved real technique. There was no lying about it; either it had separated and looked kind of curdled because you had done it wrong, or it was light and beautiful because you'd done it right.

Though that was a classic French sauce, I didn't really place it within the context of a country. My love affair with France truly started with my first job outside my mother's restaurant, in 1976. I worked for a French chef in Newport, Rhode Island, at a restaurant called The Clarke Cooke House, which is on Bannister's Wharf. Working in a classic brigade, in a very busy and very high-profile restaurant was an extraordinary experience. All of a sudden I was hearing the names of sauces and garnishes such as Veronique, Dugléré, and Chasseur, and I understood that French-trained chefs could communicate orders with a single word. And again I also learned that there was a right way to do things. We would do a *glaçage* on certain dishes, which is a hard thing to do. We'd place a sauced platter under a broiler and let it brown. If you did it right, the dish came out a beautiful golden color; if you did it wrong, it came out burnt.

But it was Roland Henin who would connect French cooking to an emotion. This was my second season in the Northeast and I was in Narragansett, Rhode Island, at a private club called the Dunes Club. He lent me his copy of Fernand Point's *Ma Gastronomie,* and its effect on me was extraordinary. I found recipes, such as one for morels with truffles, to be classic and perfect. There were lovely pictures of the garden at Point's restaurant, La Pyramide, with the chestnut trees in autumn foliage, and pictures of the dust-covered bottles in the cellar and reproductions of specific menus that Point had cooked. I lived in Newport, and I'd read the book in my apartment at night. In fact, I carried it for years, and it went up and down the coast with me, because I would go to Florida in the winter and back to work in Newport in the summer. Eventually I did give it back to him when I got my own copy. The book spoke to me about how you make food your own; it wasn't just the recipe but the idea of a dish. It brought out a desire to really understand what I was doing with food. And it helped me to understand that offering a great restaurant experience required feeling that you had been given a purpose by cooking. That was the extension.

I was partner with Serge Raoul in Rakel, in New York, from 1985 to 1990. It was located in SoHo and certainly had an element that was relaxed about it, but we also wanted it to be considered among the best restaurants in the city. We got good press, including the cover of *New York Magazine,* and I developed some signature dishes that were elegant while still retaining a little rustic edge. We did a dish called beets and leeks, and cod with a cassoulet of white beans, and we also did tuna au poivre, in which we crusted the tuna with cracked peppercorns and fanned it out in that "fine dining" way of the time. The economy, however, was against us, and eventually Serge and I agreed that the restaurant had a better chance serving casual bistro fare. I didn't want to do bistro food at the time, so I decided to leave. The decision was heartbreaking. It was my first restaurant in New York, and I'd failed. That's a pretty devastating thing.

Shortly before leaving New York for a new job at Checker's Hotel in Los Angeles, I was in Baskin-Robbins having an ice cream when I had one of those strange chef moments when you're looking at something you know as if you'd never really seen it before. I get handed my cone and my mind is suddenly whirring, trying to figure out what could be an ice cream cone's culinary adaptation. Eventually that would become an amuse-bouche, a crisp cornet which we make with our own special batter and top with prime salmon tartare.

Inspiration can strike anywhere. And as an American chef, I really do mean anywhere. I'm a guy whose grandparents were Polish, and I'd tasted a lot of Central European food long before I'd tasted anything French. I'd eaten a lot of hamburgers, too. In good food there's often something that is being figured out. There is a question and, when the dish works, a resolution. As a chef, you have to be aware of that. What are the memories here? What are the reference points? Cooking, after all, is product and execution. What makes your food yours is the experiences that you bring.

The first time I saw The French Laundry, I knew that I had found a place that was going to be important in my life. I had come up to the Napa Valley with a friend who was in the wine business and I'd dropped in to say hello to Jonathan Waxman, who was opening Table 29. He said that Don and Sally Schmitt's restaurant was available. I'd heard of the restaurant but I couldn't picture what it was like, and so, even though it was a day that the restaurant was closed, I decided to drive over and

take a look. It was evening when I got there. The whole property was bathed in a soft autumn light. It wasn't grand—the building was originally constructed as a saloon-cum-bordello in very much a boomtown spirit—but it had acquired a sense of permanence. The stone building and surrounding wall felt like they'd been there forever. There were beautiful hedges, and a Japanese maple and a crape myrtle and a gorgeous Chinese hackberry tree right by the front door.

I just walked around the property and felt an immediate emotional connection to it. I felt like I was drawn in, even without seeing the inside. "This is it," I remember thinking. "This is the place I've been looking for. This is home."

There were many traditions that Don and Sally had instituted that I liked and kept. As they had done, I wanted the garden to be part of the experience of the restaurant and for people to walk around before or after, or sometimes even during, the meal. We also kept the tradition of having a set menu. Don and Sally had started out around the same time as Chez Panisse and they, too, offered a single set menu, which allowed them to deliver a cohesive aesthetic experience. We continued that tradition also, and we expanded on it by offering a choice with each course. Gradually that evolved into offering a tasting menu, which, together with the vegetable menu, is what we offer now.

149

I find the size of portions in a tasting menu give customers just a perfect amount of food. We want them to finish each course wishing they had just one more bite. What's exciting about a tasting menu from a cook's point of view is that you're shaping a single experience over many courses. You're not just playing with tones, but with half-tones as well. We have a no-repetition rule, for example, where no ingredient can be served twice—well, perhaps with the exception of truffles—to maintain a constant sense of excitement. We're also very careful how we modulate the strength of the flavors, so over several meat courses we might just spoon some perfect consommé over the first one, the second might have a *jus*, and perhaps only the third one would be accompanied by a true sauce. Our challenge as cooks is to create dishes that have a modern sensibility (such as the oysters and pearls appetizer or even the clarified Bordelaise vinaigrette) but that always strive for the refinement, delicacy, and proportion that lie at the heart of classic French cooking.

I was approached to do Per Se as the anchor restaurant of a prestigious group of restaurants that were going to go into the Time-Warner Center. An old customer from Rakel knew one of the developers, and he said, "Call Keller. He's at The French Laundry," and it started just like that. The fact that it was going to be in a large development that had many parts and many uses didn't faze me at all. The modern chef is going to be increasingly presented with opportunities that come out of the ever-changing look of our cities. I think it's a good thing; it keeps both the restaurant and the environment feeling vibrant. My concern was, how would the standards that we set for ourselves be met?

To illustrate what goes into The French Laundry, I invited the developers to come out to Yountville and to see it for themselves. We didn't just look at the restaurant; I walked them around the town so they could see the support system behind it. They got to see the concierge offices, the human resources offices, the glassware storerooms, and the storage rooms where we keep a duplicate of every piece of machine we use so that if one breaks down we can use a replacement while we send the other to get fixed. I intended that the visit help them understand that it couldn't be just a question of getting a chef with a name and having a pretty room. To do the restaurant that we all wanted they had to share in the approach to quality that we had. And it worked. When I'd say that if we were going to have private dining I'd need a second kitchen that wouldn't hinder the work of the restaurant kitchen, there was never any question it wouldn't get built. They understood our commitment by then and they matched it.

What I always strive for is to put the people that work with me in a position where they have everything they need to succeed. While that certainly includes space and equipment, the greatest tool that I can share with people is one of attitude. Yes, I am a classicist, but that doesn't just mean how I approach food but also how I approach the craft of cooking. I wear a blue apron during *mise en place* because that is a symbol of the working cook, and I never want to lose that side of it.

There is a heritage of skills that we as cooks can choose to preserve. Every time we make a beautiful consommé, perfect puff pastry, or a magnificent high soufflé, we are making sure that certain skills and techniques survive. We give them life in a modern restaurant, and in so doing we are linked to generations of cooks that have done those same things before us. That is a feeling that I like.

But classicism goes even deeper than that. It ultimately pertains to that moment at the cutting board when you're before the ingredient.

The best ingredients can humble you. Whether it's summer peaches, wild mushrooms, or a side of Elysian Fields lamb, whenever I see great raw products brought in the back door of our kitchen I want to do something with them for our guests that will call on all that I have learned as a chef. The ingredient is already great; as a cook you can elevate that through the skill of your hands. Young cooks often want to learn one thing and then rush off and learn another. But cooking is repetition, and if being a classicist means anything, it is understanding that you are liberated by repetition. You do something often enough until it frees you. The gesture becomes automatic, and that is the moment when you can really do justice to the ingredient before you. To apply yourself to learning those skills that will liberate you is to say that in the moment of creation—the famous French *coup de feu*—you don't want any technical hurdle to come between you and what you are cooking.

Years ago, when my friend and I cleaned and scrubbed the kitchen of the Palm Beach Yacht Club, we were making it our own. We scrubbed the little nooks that you can find around a kitchen that are hard to get to, and in so doing we became, if only for that summer, more than two guys passing through. It is part of the mystery of restaurants that in such actions you become part of a place and a place becomes part of you. And that is something that I feel is important to communicate to our young cooks. This is not just a kitchen where you're practicing away what you'll one day do in your own restaurant. What you are doing here, in whatever one of my restaurants that might be—the way you act and behave and apply yourself—becomes part of this place.

That is something that I first understood as an exhausted cook looking at the pages of Fernand Point's book. There were recipes named for the Aga Khan; there were also recipes named for Point's butcher in

Vienne and for the cellar man at La Pyramide. Lots of people go into making a restaurant. I still remember many of the aphorisms that were included in Point's book. "Butter! Give me butter! Always butter!" reflects the deeply French generosity of the man. And I am reminded of the wisdom of the one that goes, "The most difficult dishes to make generally appear to be the simplest," on a daily basis when we make mashed potatoes. Their great airiness requires cooking the potatoes in their jackets, making sure they're hot as you scoop them, creating an emulsion with either chicken stock or cream that will allow you to get as much butter into the potatoes as possible. That's without even getting into how to adjust for evaporation during the service.

But my favorite one is the one that says, "A good apprentice cook must be as polite with the dishwasher as with the chef." That strikes me as profound; luxury starts right there. I am happy to be able to provide a feeling of luxuriousness in people's lives; it would be a sad day if those moments no longer existed. But I don't for a moment believe luxury is the sum of beautiful china, great wines, and fine food. For it to have a lasting meaning it has to have a human dimension, and that derives from the efforts of the people who come together to make a place unique. I really believe that you're always moving in a direction in your life, and you begin to understand the direction as you move through it. Sometimes I look at the garden of The French Laundry: the Chinese huckleberry tree might be in bloom, the antique rose bushes that Sally Schmitt planted are flowering, and the leaves of the bay laurel that I planted are catching a breeze. People are wandering around with bottles of wine, cooks are preparing food in the kitchen, and I see what I'm about. I am proud to be a cook, and I am honored to be able to provide a feeling of luxuriousness that has a human dimension at its core.

Patrick O'Connell

Patrick O'Connell is the founder of The Inn at Little Washington, in Washington, Virginia. His restaurant received the James Beard Foundation Award for Best Restaurant, as well as five stars from Mobil and five diamonds from AAA. He has published two cookbooks, *Patrick O'Connell's Refined American Cuisine* and *The Inn at Little Washington Cookbook*.

I've always believed in the idea that each of us has a particular place in the universe where we belong, and that if we find it everything will fall into place and we will flourish. For me, that place was the Blue Ridge Mountains of Virginia—the little pocket of Appalachia where I eventually opened The Inn at Little Washington.

As a young man it was very difficult for me to decide what kind of career I wanted to pursue. I had a great interest in architecture and I was going in that direction, but then I found out it involved numbers. You had to add, subtract, multiply, divide, and so that became problematic for me. Then I thought acting was fun, because I'd been in plays since first grade, but it seemed hard to take seriously as a real career. I realize now that I was fighting something, because even then I knew what I loved, and that was to cook.

My first paying job had been in a restaurant, and I had loved everything about it. It was a little carryout in southern Maryland, outside Washington, D.C. It was pre-McDonald's, and everything was still made from scratch, and it was staffed with old-time restaurant people, and, as we all know, they are a unique breed. They have a wonderful sense of humor and they're vulnerable and open and they're living in the moment. I quickly sensed that this is the culture I belonged in. There were many parallels to the world of theater—the necessity of creating an illusion, for example—but there were distinct advantages. I found the physicality therapeutic and very anchoring. Food has a way of connecting and grounding one to reality, which helps keep me centered. When you're having a really fractured day and you think you can't deal with it anymore, you can just get a big batch of dough going and stick your fingers in it and suddenly everything's better. Or you make some cookies and fill the atmosphere with their wonderful aromas and you're back—you're okay.

I had had it with getting bitten by dogs on my paper route, so one summer day I rode my bike to this carryout in our little town and walked up and knocked on the screen door of the kitchen. I still have a recurring nightmare about the screen door—that I'm still looking for that job. So in my dream I knock at the screen door, and an old restaurant geezer opens it and gives me this "What the hell do you want?" look and then asks, "Can you cook?" There are beads of sweat on my forehead, and I say, "Yeah." Then he says, "Can you make a minestrone soup?" And I think, "I'm sure I could make a minestrone soup." I really think I could do it. I guess that screen door left a rather indelible impression and sort of changed my life. But the restaurant owner took me in, and I worked a summer there and was just in heaven.

So, the following summer, I went back, knocked on the screen door again, and the owner said, "What are you doing here?" and I said, "I want my job back." And he said, "Well, you can't work in this dump. You've got to go somewhere better. I've got a friend who has a restaurant with tablecloths." There was no turning back from that point. But at the end of that summer, I went to college to appease my parents. I studied theater, but it felt stilted and artificial, and all the people were self-absorbed basket cases. I realized that the "living theater" of the restaurant business was more exciting than the real theater. It was spontaneous and like watching two shows at once—the fantasy out front and the blood and guts going on in the kitchen in the back—a sort of surreal juxtaposition.

I needed to figure out what I wanted to do with my life, so I quit school and took a year off and decided to travel around Europe to clear my mind. Before embarking on my journey, a wise friend encouraged me to buy a little piece of property way out in the Virginia countryside so I'd be sure to have a place to come back to and not spend every last cent I'd saved. So I bought a little place on two and a half acres in an Appalachian hollow inhabited by one mountain family who were feuding. It was a mountain shack with a school bus attached to the rear, an outhouse, and eight wrecked cars decorating the front yard. Later I found out that if the sheriff was ever called to come to Jenkins Hollow, he'd refuse to come. This was a particularly colorful era in America—the late sixties and early seventies. Some young people believed in the concept of early retirement, while they could still enjoy it. This was the happiest time of my life when I realized that I had found my place in the universe.

157

After returning from my European journey with a much deeper appreciation of the potential for artistic fulfillment as a chef, I sold the shack to some hippies who added a geodesic dome onto the side of it and I bought a larger farmhouse on the other side of the mountain. I cooked night and day. I'd cook anything I could get my hands on. Friends would joke that even people's pets weren't safe.

My original idea was to open a restaurant in the farmhouse, because very frequently I'd look up from the dinner table and count fourteen people dining with us who had just stopped by or driven out from the city for the day. They were usually ravenous, and after every meal somebody would invariably say, "You should open a restaurant." My partner wisely objected to turning our home into a restaurant, so, instead, we rented half of an abandoned gas station in a nearby town of Washington, Virginia (affectionately known as "Little Washington"), seventeen miles closer to Washington, D.C. It came with a junk-yard, an outhouse, and a bat-infested upstairs. The town dump was in the rear. Our rent was two hundred dollars per month. Fortunately we had an option to purchase the building at the end of the first year.

Every night guests still want to know how I discovered this remote location, and I explain that my parents had their honeymoon in the next town over the mountain. They came out here on a Greyhound bus to a romantic old mountain hotel. When we were children, living in the Washington, D.C., suburbs, we used to drive out to the mountains to have Sunday dinner at the old hotel where they'd honeymooned. I fell in love with the idea of going out to the country and setting aside a whole day for a beautiful meal.

The Inn at Little Washington started humbly. The local people were saying, "Well, what are they doing this for? Who do they think is coming to this place?" We knew that weeknights were going to be very difficult; however, we could probably count on some of the people whom we knew in the area to come on Saturday nights. So the plan was if it was slim pickings, my partner would work at a restaurant in Washington, D.C., in the front of the house as a waiter, and I would work in the kitchen and also serve during the week. He would come home on Friday, Saturday, and Sunday and actually work in the dining room.

So the first night we opened, we had seventy-five guests, and I had one boy in the kitchen who lied about his age. He said he was fifteen, but he was fourteen. The kitchen was designed like a real kitchen, but I had to run around from one station to the other. So it was a little startling, and what was even more startling was that unlike the catering business, this wasn't going to stop. So there was this constant thing of how long do I have to do this? Is this ever going to end? And, of course, it doesn't. It's a lifestyle. It's a life's work. It's an addiction, an obsession, and a passion.

159

Our labor pool was either local high school girls or older women who'd worked in the area's sewing plant that had closed. So not one of our first staff had ever stepped foot in a restaurant in their lives before. We soon found out that we were so busy we couldn't go the fourteen miles to our old farmhouse at night. We had to stay in a fleabag motel at the foot of the hill, which was also occupied by two country prostitutes next door. So we would open around seven in the morning and leave around one thirty. I wrote the menu on a mimeograph machine, by hand, and then if I made an error, I scraped it off with a razor blade. Then I did the flowers and got myself organized to run a restaurant.

Everything was complicated. The bread delivery was timed with the laundry. Both were dropped off outside at another restaurant about thirty miles away. So we had to go to that restaurant's back door, where there would be the pile of laundry in canvas bags and shopping bags of bread for us. Now, when it snowed or it rained, they wouldn't put it inside, so you had to watch the weather forecast and you had to time it just right to get there.

We got produce where we could find it. I went to a Chinese restaurant in a nearby town before opening to find out how we could share some of the delivery things. I wanted some snow peas and things like that, and I said, "How often does the delivery truck come out from Washington, D.C.," and they said, "Once a month." And I said, "No, no, no. Not the canned stuff. I mean your fresh stuff, your little snow peas. How often does the delivery come?" "Once a month." Talk about having to be creative.

I did a cooking demonstration in Washington, D.C., and in the audience was a purveyor, and he said, "Where do you guys get your fish?" And I said, "We drive into the city and go to the market and pick it up." He said, "Why didn't you call me? I'll come out." And I said, "Gee, nobody in the past ever would come near us." They didn't actually believe that such a place existed, and the peculiar name, Washington, Virginia, created confusion. They said, "Make up your mind, buddy. You're either in one or the other. You can't be in both of those places at the same time." So he was our first delivery person. I then had other purveyors deliver to the fish guy, and then he would come out with everything.

I always tell my guests that in my next lifetime I fully intend to do it right and go to culinary school, because it's much harder if you don't know how. But in truth it isn't about a school but about the receptivity of the student and how badly they want this information. Now, a great teacher can sometimes ignite the spark, but you have to have a goal. You have to have a dream. It's that simple. It's not a passive exercise. I think a problem in this culture, with education, is we think it's a filling-up, like having your tank topped off or something, but it really doesn't work that way. It's about your falling in love with it and melding and obsessing. Many people think they go to school, sit in a chair, take notes, pass a test, and they've got it. But you have to become your teacher and walk in that person's shoes to actually get it.

Early on I understood the importance of reference points, so I think if I have one great piece of advice for young people, it is to establish those. Find the greatest restaurant in the world and study it. Don't be intimidated by someone else's success, but realize that if it's humanly possible, you, too, can do it, provided you're willing to make major sacrifices. The turning point for me was that after one year of being opened with dinner at $4.95, I, with my partner, went to eat in some of the great European restaurants that we'd read so much about. Each one of them that I visited, dinner cost more than our car. And it was sort of unthinkable that you were taking your last pennies of a year's earnings and eating, but it was the best education I ever had. It wasn't just the food. I was establishing a clear reference point and a measuring stick of where I was in relation to the purportedly greatest restaurants in the world. So at first it was like a trip to Mars, and then I realized it was so beneficial. I did it on a regular basis every year, and after about seventeen, eighteen, years of watching the gap between what they were doing, particularly the French, and what I was doing, you watched the gap narrow, until one day there was no more gap.

Today I feel that my role is to represent the client or the guest in our restaurant. Many young culinarians really don't know who their audience is. In reality, the people had a magnificent meal at a business lunch and they've dined out three times that week. They're jaded. They're cranky. They're sitting down and they're saying, "Astonish me," and, "I'm not hungry." They don't want a mountain of food. They're picky. They're irritable. You have to know who they are.

So I keep after the staff. When you reach a certain point, it becomes enormously harder to push it up from there. It's very easy when you're a gas station, you know, to go whoosh, and then you get at a certain level, but then it becomes Herculean to go a little bit higher. So I walk in, and the very first thing I see is the flaws, and so I tell the managers and the key people, "Did you find your thirty flaws yet?" And they say, "Don't worry. I found fifty." It's this idea of bringing everyone up to operate at a level beyond what they really want to operate on, and then there has to be something in it for them. The ultimate payoff is an attitude. Contact with great quality changes people; you look at the world differently. I've seen it happen with many of our employees.

The flip side of that, perhaps even the tragedy of our business, is you develop such an acute, critical faculty that you train yourself to only see what's wrong. In one's own restaurant it might be necessary, but I feel when we go out we really should learn to let it go. What is most important is the intimacy that food allows. Looking at a plate of food or eating is just like reading a book. Everything is revealed. The creator of the dish; there's nothing to hide behind. If you're astute and tuned into it, and do this regularly, you can write a small biography of the person who made the dish. You know their reference points, you know if they have European training, you know pretty much what region they're from, and they may not even be conscious that they're exposing this aspect of themselves.

I don't believe in accidents. I don't believe that we intersect in life accidentally. I believe there's meaning in all of our interactions. I believe that customers really want to connect with me, and my hope is that I'll have a chance to connect with them. Our humanness is in the details, and our challenge is to be able to express that within the crazy pressure of a restaurant.

The next challenge for chefs is to address their art as part of a healing process and to recognize that we have the power to offer that to people. We can invigorate sensations grown tired by the everyday; we can slow down time and allow people to share in an unforgettable moment. And yet we must offer all this within a context that is unforgiving, where no matter how long you've been cooking, you must prove yourself with each dish. There is no track record in restaurants, just as there's no cumulative reward. You can't lie to people's palates and that is precisely what makes the restaurant experience feel so vital. People might be walking out of our restaurants at night, but when it works, they can feel like it's a bright new day.

Charlie Palmer

Raised on a farm in upstate New York, Charlie Palmer trained in the kitchens of the best French restaurants in New York City. His first restaurant, Aureole, opened in New York, with several more to follow there and in Washington, D.C., and Las Vegas. He now has eleven restaurants and is the author of three cookbooks.

I grew up in the small town of Smyrna, New York. My father was a farmer, a plumber, an electrician, and a jack-of-all-trades—he could fix anything. I had a great childhood and while we always had everything we wanted, I could never figure out how my father supported our family on the money he made. I think there was a lot of barter going on.

By the age of fourteen, I was six feet tall and wanted to be a professional football player. There's no shortage of high school players who envision themselves in the pros, and reality set in during my junior year when I realized the small percentage of athletes who can actually get to that level. It was about this same time that I got interested in cooking. Our neighbor Sharon Crane was the Home Ec teacher, and I noticed that a lot of great food came out of her kitchen. When I started asking her questions, she made me an irresistible offer. "Take Home Ec, and you won't have to sew," she said. "You will only cook and get to eat anything you want." That sounded pretty enticing to a growing guy, and after forcing six of my friends to sign up as well, I was in.

As you can imagine, it was pretty tame. Mostly we baked. But since I also did a lot of hunting and fishing, I'd bring in what I caught and we'd cook it. Before long I was thinking that here was something I would like to do. At the time, it wasn't a question of being a "chef"— the word *chef* didn't come into it. Whether you cooked at a restaurant or a diner, you were essentially a laborer. I had older brothers who all looked at me like, "You're going to cook? What are you talking about?" Believe me, they're much more receptive to the idea now.

By the time I was a senior in high school, I was completely into cooking and sports simultaneously. I had an old copy of the *Larousse Gastronomique* that Sharon had given me, and I'd say, "Ooh, so that's a *pithiviers*." I also played football at 250, 260 pounds, and then I'd have to get down to 215 in three weeks to wrestle, so out came the rubber suit. But in hindsight, it was good training; once you've done high school wrestling, no kitchen seems tough.

Only when I got into culinary school did I really understand the possibilities that professional cooking offered. I've always been the kind of person who believes anything can happen. My father told me there's no limit to what a person can do. "Don't think you have to be a certain way," he'd say. "And don't listen to anybody who tells you that you can't do something. You can; it's up to you." So pretty early on, I made the decision to have my own restaurant and was determined that it was going to happen. The most important thing was to plan out how I was going to get to that point and be ready for it.

The first step was to get a foundational education, which I did at The Culinary Institute of America, in Hyde Park. I became very close to my instructor, Leon Dhaenens, a Belgian chef who had worked in the city at the Colony and other places. We would cater parties on weekends and work together. He was my mentor and communicated his real passion for food to me. When you grow up in this country, I don't think there's really that much passion put into food. Everybody in my family loved to eat; the actual food wasn't of that much importance. With Dhaenens, it was always about discovering new things and eating different food. I had never eaten caviar, so he wanted to make sure that I tasted it.

When it was time to start looking for a job, he brought me to New York. I will always remember that we had lunch at Jean-Jacques Rachou's restaurant Le Lavandou, which was a huge deal for me. It was a real French restaurant, very well known and highly regarded at the time. I remember exactly what I had: Dover sole with a kind of *calvados beurre blanc* and apples *risoles* and little puff pastry *fleurons*. Very creative at that time. I had a little casserole of sweetbreads to start. Afterward Jean-Jacques came out, and he and Dhaenens spoke French—I had no idea what they were saying. Then Jean-Jacques shook my hand and said, "Okay, you start in two weeks." That's how I got in. I had no idea what I was doing, no idea if I was getting paid. But I answered, "I'll be there. What time?" That was it.

Kitchens were run differently back then: There were no set hours. You just worked until there was no more work. I started as a butcher and *charcutier* at La Côte Basque, learning from a really great French-trained charcuterie expert—a great sausage maker. And then, at nighttime, I did a lot of pastry. I worked probably at least eighteen hours a day, for the most part. In the summertime, I also worked in other restaurants.

One great thing about being a young American in French kitchens was that the French guys always went on long vacations during the summer. They would take four to six weeks, and chefs would phone around to find people to stand in, like a *poissonnier* to work nights at Le Chantilly. A group of us shuffled around from kitchen to kitchen, making one hundred bucks a shift, which at that time was a lot of money. Working for all these different chefs was great experience, and there was a real sense of camaraderie.

I then did a stint at a small country club, the Waccabuc Country Club in Waccabuc, New York. I relish my time there because it was like cooking in a capsule: I could do anything I wanted. In many country clubs, the members might not care what they eat, but these people did. They didn't want club chow. It was almost like a laboratory. During this year of my kitchen life, I found my voice as a cook and developed the style I would become known for—progressive American cooking.

I have a problem with the term *American cuisine* because it's still not established. A cuisine is not something that happens in fifteen or twenty years, or even fifty years, you know. French cuisine is a true cuisine because it's been such a long period of time. So we're progressive and we're American—I find that works.

At twenty-four, I became the executive chef at the River Café—although I was not really ready to be. But I was a very good actor, and this was an incredible opportunity; I would make it happen no matter what. I was always smart enough to surround myself with great people, and I still believe that's such a huge part of what we do in this business. So I had a great team and knew what I wanted to do in terms of food. Then we just made it happen every night on a very visible platform.

But food was changing. Most of the classical French cooking that I had done prior to this relied on a lot of cream and butter. When you're using those ingredients in quantity, you're buffering flavor—not enhancing it. Now, my idea was to keep an ingredient as pure as possible and *pull* flavor out of it. If you're going to have squab, I want it to taste like squab, not masked by too much flavor. I'd take squab stock and reduce it down to where it's really, really intense, and maybe add the essence of red wine or shallots. At the end of the day it's about the squab. It's still about what you're cooking, and that was really important and a very big part of what we called the big picture—the big philosophy.

In the late eighties, when I was twenty-eight, it was finally time for me to open the restaurant I had been designing over and over again in my head. There was a little bit of a competition about what to call it, and the name Aureole came from a good friend of mine, a professor at NYU. I was looking for a name that would become known as a restaurant—like Lutèce. Not many people know it comes from the Romans' name for Paris [Lutetia]. When you said "Lutèce," people automatically responded, "Oh, the French restaurant on Fiftieth Street." That's exactly what I wanted: a big-time restaurant that could compete with the great restaurants of New York. I knew it had to be Upper East Side, Midtown. It had to be close to Fifth Avenue. I really wanted it to be a town house because I wanted that town house "feel." I wanted to be the American Lutèce and establish American cooking in my town house just like André Soltner had done with French cuisine in his.

But that was so easy to say. It was '87 to '88 when I decided to do Aureole—the days of Black Monday, when the stock market crashed. And everybody was looking at me like, "Okay, so you're going to open a high-end restaurant on the Upper East Side with a big-ticket average in the worst economy that's happened in what, twenty-five years?" And I'd say, "Yeah, I can make it happen." I was very confident, plus I had nothing to lose. I already knew how to live poor, so what's the worst that could happen?

Understandably, it took me a little while to find a financial partner who shared my idea. I met with a number of people who were interested. You see, I was looking for one investor, not a group. I approached each potential investor with my plan: I wanted to play with the big guys because I just felt like that's where I needed to be. If an investor didn't agree, I'd move on. I had a very specific thing that I wanted to do, and if I could do exactly that, I knew I would be successful.

Eventually I got the financing in place, and suddenly I was the owner of a restaurant. That's when I started finding out all sorts of things: that not everybody loves you and that you actually have to know something about business. At that point, I wasn't sure if the money we were making was getting into the bank. I also learned that when you're a cook, you really need someone you trust to manage what goes on in the front of the house—which I had and still have in Alex Gouras. I even learned a thing or two about old New York brownstones. Two days before the restaurant was to open, a two-inch water line broke and flooded the entire building; the new wood floors just buckled up. It was just a disaster. But two days later, when we had it mostly fixed and could open the restaurant on time, I was very pleased. It was just amazing that we did that, because we'd had cooks out there tearing up wood floors.

People can make a living with a single restaurant if they're smart. The big misconception is that restaurants are a way to make a lot of money. The profit margins are small. I think if you do a bang-up job, you can do ten percent. However, the margins are shrinking, because you can only charge so much, yet products continue to get pricier. We're as affected by gas prices as any other industry. But perhaps the biggest issue facing chefs today is the confusing concept of multiple restaurants. Many people—from the working press to paying customers— just assume that when a chef has more than one restaurant, it can't be great. I beg to differ; if I was cooking at Aureole for eighteen years now without changing, you wouldn't want to eat there. I would feel caught up in a daily grind, and I just don't think that's the way life should be. And it's not as though we're all out there really duplicating places. Once you start doing the cookie-cutter type of thing, then you're not talking about what I would call a "real" restaurant. Frankly, very few people who approach you to open a restaurant want a copy. They're buying a brand. They think your brand will enhance their property and vice versa. Once you get into that, you're in a partnership.

I looked at Las Vegas for about two years before we opened an Aureole there. I thought, if we're going to do another restaurant, it could be in Chicago or San Francisco, but there are already a lot of great restaurants there. At the time, Las Vegas was underserved—hard to believe. Only Emeril and Wolfgang had restaurants there; everything else was buffets. So it was a chance to be on the forefront. How many times in life do you get to be a pioneer?

I looked at a number of different situations and eventually I met Bill Richardson. He's from Vegas but is a very un-Vegas guy. He convinced me that the Mandalay Bay was where I should be to have a chance to do something that probably couldn't be done elsewhere. I couldn't find that kind of physical space in New York City or any other metropolitan area. I got a huge kitchen and a forty-three-foot wine tower that holds ten thousand bottles. And there are live wine angels rappelling up and down retrieving the wine.

You can build incredibly beautiful restaurants and spend millions of dollars and build towers and all these things, but at the end of the day it's about the people you surround yourself with and work with. I always put myself in their position. I wouldn't want to be in a job where I'm not growing. If I'm going to grow, they're going to grow. That's the way I look at it, and I think it's the only way to promote a healthy business that's going to sustain itself for twenty or more years. I just don't see any other way to do it.

A great deal of the restaurant business today is entertainment: the way someone feels in a restaurant and the way they perceive the place itself before they even put a bite of food in their mouths. Today I'm part of that entertainment-oriented world. But at the same time I can miss the days when I just cooked, wiped down my station, and put my knives away. The kitchen has changed. The stakes are higher and the cooks have more training. It's not like the old days, when the chef would throw stuff at me and I would duck. I can remember Jean-Jacques Rachou firing plates at me. You can't do that anymore.

But it gives me a lot of satisfaction to know I am a link in a chain. I have a great respect for that generation of chefs, like André Soltner and Alain Sailhac and Jean-Jacques Rachou and Roland Chenus. I have great respect for that kind of worldly attitude that they first brought to this country, because they lived it and changed how we think about food. Ideally, in ten years time, people will look back at my generation of chefs and think that we changed how people think about restaurants. The world is evolving; everything's changing. Restaurants are like everything else. They have to evolve, too.

Jacques Pépin

Born near Lyon, Jacques Pépin was first exposed to the world of cooking at his parents' restaurant. At age thirteen he began an apprenticeship in his hometown at the Grand Hôtel de l'Europe. He trained under Lucien Diat at the Plaza Athénée in Paris and served as personal chef to French heads of state, including Charles de Gaulle. He moved to the United States in 1959 to work at Le Pavillon in New York and then became the director of research and development for the Howard Johnson Company, where he worked for ten years. Pépin has published several cookbooks and hosted numerous cooking shows, including *Julia and Jacques Cooking at Home*. Pépin has been the dean of special programs at The French Culinary Institute since 1988. His memoir, *The Apprentice*, was a national bestseller.

When I first came to America I thought I was working half a day. At Le Pavillon, only the executive chef worked two shifts. I started in the morning and then I worked the night shift. So I'd finish at three in the afternoon and then I was off. This was incredible compared to the way it was in France. My friend Jean-Claude Szurdak, who'd worked with me for the French president, and another guy who worked with me at Le Pavillon had an apartment above a restaurant called La Toque Blanche, on Fiftieth Street. We had three windows in the front, three in the back. We had the whole floor. Three private entrances to get into the apartment. Each one had a bedroom, a living room, a kitchen, and a bath. We paid seventy-five dollars a month split three ways. Even earning eighty dollars a week at Le Pavillon, I was fine.

There was a lot of mishmash in the French restaurant world at the time. In most of the Theater District or West Side restaurants the cooks were invariably from Brittany, so what might pass for a regional specialty such as cassoulet was at best an approximation by someone who might never have eaten the real thing. Le Pavillon was more expensive than these places by many multiples; but there were other expensive French restaurants at the time. What made Le Pavillon different was that it was the real thing. Whether it was an omelet at lunchtime or bass with champagne sauce, the food was sophisticated, classic, clear, and light in that way that French food can be when it is done with attention.

I fit in well. My childhood in Bourg-en-Bresse, a region of great raw products, had allowed me to understand culinary quality early. Nevertheless, I have never romanticized what a French culinary apprenticeship was. When I started cooking, at thirteen, you had to steal the trade. No one really took time for you. For one year you cleaned and took care to keep the stove hot. If the stove wasn't hot, it was a disaster. One day the chef says, "You start at the stove tomorrow," and you'd better have been watching, because no one is going to be there to hold your hand. That system may have led to great high points but, frankly, it also led to harsh, demanding, and unyielding chefs, difficult to work with and too rigid.

Still, it had allowed me to cook for De Gaulle, travel to America, easily enter the kitchen of the country's best restaurant, and get to know this amazing city I'd read so much about: New York. We used to go dancing on Eighty-sixth Street in the German dance halls in Yorkville between Second and Third avenues. There were restaurants on every street selling sausage and sauerkraut, and the dance halls were one of the few places—certainly that we knew about—that you could invite a girl at another table to dance like we do in France. It was a great time. Though I worked in what was considered the best restaurant in the country, Le Pavillon, I was less than impressed by its imperious owner, Henri Soulé. He would give a can of caviar to the Duke of Windsor but refused to raise anyone's salaries. For my friend Pierre Franey, who was the chef and who had come over with Soulé to work at the 1939 World's Fair, enough was enough, and eventually he left. When I said that the rest of the kitchen should leave with him, I got a visit from two big guys from Local 86, the union we belonged to that represented dishwashers and cooks. They held me up against the locker and said some things that I couldn't make out but that I understood perfectly well. If the schedules were new to me, this was new, too.

Eventually I joined Pierre working at research and development at Howard Johnson headquarters out in Queens Village. Mr. Johnson had been a customer of Le Pavillon and he was a true connoisseur of food and he wanted to make the food at his restaurants better. This was a huge company. At the time it was bigger than McDonald's, Burger King, and Kentucky Fried Chicken combined. So if at Le Pavillon, Pierre and I had been cooking for the few, we were now embarked on feeding the many. I would cook with a chemist by my side. We each had our responsibility. I, for example, had to try and figure out how to make three thousand pounds of beef bourguignon. Their job was to analyze concepts I'd never heard of, such as the "specific gravity" of a dish.

At the same time I was studying for a BA at Columbia. I hadn't set out to do this, and originally I only wanted to take a course of English for foreign students. One course led to another, and I was finally so deeply involved in my studies that after work at Howard Johnson I'd rush over the Triborough Bridge in my little car so as to get to the night courses on time. Having an education helped me in many ways, but perhaps the greatest was one of my own self-perception. It prevented me from having a complex about not having an education. I come from a generation of French cooks that left school at thirteen, and that complex is more prevalent than many of us cared to admit.

When Mr. Johnson died the company started cutting back, and the effects were dreadful. It wasn't an overnight change; it was incremental—the way a loss of quality usually happens. Originally, if we'd wanted to make five thousand cans of chowder in one batch, we might use five hundred pounds of onions. But someone would change the quantities to only four hundred pounds of real onion with the addition of ten pounds of dehydrated onions. You taste that, it tastes practically the same. So you take another twenty pounds of onions and instead of putting three hundred pounds of butter in the roux you put in two hundred and add fifty of margarine. Again you don't see the difference, and you keep not seeing the difference between successive versions, except the difference between the first and the eighth version is enormous.

In 1970, I left Howard Johnson and opened La Potagerie, on Fifth Avenue. I couldn't have opened this restaurant if I hadn't worked at Howard Johnson. Mass production and the organization of recipes had always appealed to my rather Cartesian mind. Not to mention that a thorough knowledge of food was necessary for the volume we were doing. We sat 102 people, and we once did 912 people for lunch between eleven and three. That's a turnover every seventeen minutes. That's volume. Joe Baum, one of the legends of the American restaurant business (he started Restaurant Associates and the Four Seasons), came to see me one day and asked me if I would set up the commissary for the World Trade Center. Volume didn't scare me at all by then, and I said that I would like to do that.

The buildings weren't completely finished when I went down to see him and he gave me a tour of the kitchens. The engineering firm had built everything wrong, from the huge kettles to the pumping system. I told him it was all wrong. He said, "Well, it's been approved by the Port Authority of New York, and we're not changing anything. You have to live with that." So you had these massive kettles that were too close to the ground to be tipped, and the pipes in the pumping system were so narrow that everything stuck in them. We'd make stocks with two thousand pounds of veal bones, but instead of having a crane and a basket to empty it in twenty minutes I had two guys with shovels working for four hours.

I was at a point in my career where I was cooking in kitchens involved in the mass production of food, quite far from my Paris training. I would eventually go in the direction of authorship and education with the publication of *La Technique*. It was a somewhat convoluted path to write that book. Very soon after I arrived in the U.S. I had met Craig Claiborne, the famed dining editor of the *New York Times* who would eventually collaborate with Pierre Franey on many books and columns for the *Times*. Craig was always dressed properly in the city, with a suit and tie, and had southern manners, but he also had a deep appreciation for good food. Through Craig I had met Helen McCully, a wonderfully elegant and fun Canadian who was the editor of *House Beautiful* magazine. She, in fact, had been the first person to encourage me to pursue activities related to cooking, but outside kitchens. One of those activities was stamp-size black-and-white pictures we took showing basic culinary techniques. You really couldn't see much, but we got an appreciative response and did a short series. One weekend out in East Hampton, visiting Pierre and Craig, I met Herb Nagourney, president of Times Books, and his girlfriend, Ann Bramson, who were talking to Craig about a book he was doing. At some stage Herb said to me, "Don't you want to try and do something with us?" I said, "I'd love to." "What do you have in mind?" I said, "I'd like to do a book of technique," and he said, "Great. Come to see me in my office. We'll work on that."

What I visualized was a book based on the cooking classes I had started to give, which I thought could be covered in about three hundred pictures. But my students kept asking questions, and I realized that even basic questions, like how to peel a carrot, had to be addressed. I worked with a French photographer who came to my house every couple of months, and we'd shoot a series until I knew what else I wanted to do and then he'd come back. I told Herb, "I see from my cooking classes I need more pictures, so now I have four hundred." He said, "Okay, go ahead." The next time I saw him I said, "I have eight hundred pictures." Then I'd go back to my students and they'd ask me how to skim a sauce and then I had to shoot that. At some point I had fifteen hundred pictures, and Herb said, "That's enough." So I had to stop, but I still had more ideas, and I wanted to do a second volume, which we called *La Méthode*.

One book led to another, and eventually Julia Child encouraged me to try and do television. I had to learn a whole new set of tools, like how to adapt to the time constraints and how to address the camera. Instructions like "Talk to the camera" are not exactly what I had been trained to do. I go into these details to acknowledge some of the people who have helped me, who've brought out latent talents, the people whose paths you cross who can open up entire new directions in your life. We cooks are a tightly bound group, in many ways everyone who isn't there sweating with us in the heat exists outside our world. While I love that bond, it is a mistake for young cooks to not see outside it, even in those moments when you think others have it easy. We must live in two worlds, because that is our privilege; we can and should always strive to live in the world of others, recognizing that others can't just come into the kitchen and live in ours.

It has been almost four decades since I arrived in this country. There have been many changes. When I first came there were two types of salads in the supermarkets—iceberg and romaine. Today a chef isn't going to let you out of the restaurant without having you taste fifteen types of greens. But there have been more profound changes than that. Cooks in the U.S. were very low on the social scale, lower in fact than in France, where we at least had the tradition of artisanship. Perhaps the thing I am proudest of is that in whatever way I have been able to I have helped the métier of chef become a profession of which people can be proud.

Though I am considered by many to be the quintessential Frenchman, I don't actually cook all that French. I don't think in terms of French or not French. In fact, when my mother would visit and I'd cook, she'd often say, "That was delicious; but it wasn't French." In many ways the lack of a strong national American cuisine, as well as the open-mindedness of Americans, were factors that allowed me to succeed.

I would like that people understand that the enjoyment of food demands a certain approach. For good cooking you always must go deep into the product. If you're making a French-style roast chicken, yes, making the vinaigrette with a bit of the chicken fat and putting a little bit of the *jus* into it makes a delicious accompanying salad. But if you're making a lobster roll or a BLT or a Reuben sandwich, respect the products, have a good technique, and always realize that the dish could be improved.

But true enjoyment of food also demands a bit of a surrender, the ability to relax into whatever it might bring. Ironically, it was an American, Craig Claiborne, who taught me this. Having just recently arrived from France, it was a revelation for me the way he entertained. At his home in East Hampton, you got up when you wanted, made your own coffee, and maybe a sandwich for lunch. At about three, we all got together and started to cook dinner. This was a contrast with the French way, where everything was planned. In France you didn't just go into somebody's house and open the fridge; at Craig's everyone did that; it was the most natural thing in the world. So there is that sense of living in the pleasure of the moment that cooking allows. I had spent many years cooking and I didn't understand that. The most important thing about food I learned right here.

Michel Richard

French-born, Michel Richard started his career as an apprentice at a pâtisserie in Champagne, France, and later moved to Paris, where he worked at Gaston Lenôtre's pastry shop. Richard eventually moved to Los Angeles, where he opened Michel Richard and then Citrus. He continued his restaurant expansion with Citronelle, first in Santa Barbara, then in Baltimore, Philadelphia, and Washington, D.C., where Richard now lives. He is also the author of *Michel Richard's Home Cooking with a French Accent* and *Happy in the Kitchen*.

I say I'm from the Champagne region because no one knows the Ardennes. People who knew the history of the two world wars do, but it's not a very well known part of France. Champagne is close, and everyone can locate it. I was actually born in Brittany, and after the war my parents moved to the Ardennes because the area had been destroyed and there was a lot of work. When I was eight years old, my father met a lady younger than my mother and he left us. He moved out. I don't know what happened to him.

My mother used to work at a factory, and many times I had to cook for my brother and sister. We kept rabbits, and if my mother wasn't around I'd have to kill one, hitting it on the head with a rolling pin. I far preferred going shopping for food. My mother would give me a thousand *ancien* francs, about two dollars, and with that I was able to buy four horse steaks and potatoes for French fries, and I'd have a little money left over to buy chocolate for a mousse.

A friend of mine who knew I was interested in food (because I used to watch Raymond Oliver on television) invited me to come over to see his father's restaurant. We entered through the back door, like in any kitchen in the world, and immediately I was in love with the atmosphere of the kitchen. I was ten years old, and from the owner's point of view I must have seemed unshakable. I was constantly there, doing odd jobs or asking to roll dough to make a tart. I had fallen in love with food.

There was no way I was going to stay at school, because we had no money. My mother didn't want us to go to college [middle school]. "No, no, you have to go to work," she'd say. "We need the money." I worked in a factory for six months, and I hated it. I was melting bronze. It was dirty. I finally said to my mother, "I want to be a chef." She said, "Before becoming a chef you have to be a pastry chef first. You have to learn how to bake." I didn't want to be a pastry chef, but it was close enough. It was a profession by which you could travel. I don't mean travel like being on a deck chair of a cruise ship. I mean it was a profession by which you could get out of where you were.

By the time I was eighteen I was married and a father, and if it hadn't been for that I would have stopped doing pastry. Everything was mediocre at the time. The croissant *au beurre* was made with margarine; the butter cream with margarine, too. Why do you call it butter cream if it's margarine? I would ask. They were not cutting corners. It was worse; they were impostors. What do you do after butter cream with margarine, butter cream with pork fat? And the ambiance in these stores was dismal, too; they were dark with almost no refrigeration. Can you imagine a cake spending eight hours in a window? That was the state of French baking at the time.

After my military service I moved to Paris. I was twenty-one years old and I got a job working for Gaston Lenôtre, the most legendary pâtissier in France. He's the person whose attitude kept me in baking. He was smart, charming, and he gave us the best quality to work with. The best butter, the best eggs, real vanilla beans. Before that, I had never seen a vanilla bean. I thought a vanilla bean looked like a *haricot blanc,* a dry white bean. I didn't know a vanilla bean was long.

It was at Lenôtre that I discovered I was good at this. Suddenly I was enthusiastic about the profession. I used to go home and study. I did sugar work in our tiny apartment. I trained myself to write on cakes by using toothpaste squeezed into a paper cone at home. It's all in the pressure you squeeze with, the height you work from— different heights for different effects—and your ability to come to a precise stop. In France, if you know something you don't say it; you don't want to be pretentious. You wait until the day someone asks if anyone can write on cakes, and you casually say you can. You do it and you go back to your tasks. No one says anything, but you have gone up in everyone's eyes. They know you're good.

Lenôtre sent me to the States to work at what would be an ill-fated pastry store in New York. Even if the store was to close, I learned about America through eating. In my first meals out I would look at dessert names like *cheesecake* and *carrot cake* in utter amazement. A cake made from cheese! To the French ear it didn't sound right, and yet it was deli-

187

cious. After a few months the pastry store closed, but I wasn't ready to go back to France. I wanted to learn English. People were offering me jobs in New York, but I didn't want to work in some basement kitchen trying to get to my puff pastry between a cook's legs, so when I was offered a job in Santa Fe, in a pastry shop in La Fonda hotel, I took it. I bought a small car and drove to New Mexico, and again I had another learning experience. In France we don't have crunch. During the drive I would try and eat at Kentucky Fried Chicken places because I loved the texture of that chicken—and I still do.

Santa Fe would be good for me. It gave me a sense that I could actually survive in the country outside New York. As a pastry chef, the altitude represented a real opportunity to learn. Here I was, this big pastry chef whose profiteroles and cream puffs were totally flat. But I strived for more, and eventually moved to Los Angeles and opened a pastry store there. I got back into the atmosphere of the kitchen because Lenôtre was friends with all the big chefs like Bocuse, and when they came to do dinners in the U.S., I was often asked to be the pastry chef for the night. I would see things and I would run back to my pastry store and put something new on the menu. I would turn vegetables, I would do something *en croûte,* I would try and get people to go beyond quiche, something I could maybe serve with a sauce. I was gradually coming back to what I had wanted to do first.

Gradually this cooking started to take over. I would do dinners for friends, three and four dinners a week for six people. I got to do a menu at one of the first French restaurants in L.A., Robaire's, whose owner "Papouche" Robaire allowed me to. And it seemed natural to be looking for backers. Many of the potential backers said French food was over. From décor to sauces, they thought it was tired and old. But to me French food is something living. It reflects its environment and in fact it is fascinating how it is constantly adapting. When we opened Citrus in 1986 we were completely new. The name came from the cross street it was on, but to me it had a lime-colored vibrancy. We didn't have heavy red drapes; we had cream-colored parasols. We didn't have an endless menu; it was all on one page. We didn't have a hidden kitchen you dared not approach; it was clean and filled with light and open for you to see. And most important, though I'd never actually worked in a restaurant, from the crab coleslaw to the crème brûlée Napoléon, the food was completely mine.

People often say that there are great differences between pastry chefs and chefs. There's this almost caricature that the pastry chef is always measuring and weighing. That focus is certainly necessary at the beginning, but when I'm leaning over a turning paddle of a Hobart making something, I'm not measuring anything. The knowledge is in my hands. What I do think pastry chefs have is a certain rigor, an internal sense of precision, which is a factor by which they judge. I judge a cake by its corners and how cleanly it meets the plate. Those two things show me if someone has the touch. Cooking invites you to be more poetic, to take inspiration from the product, but for me the approach is similar. When I see something that's not perfect, it hurts me so much. I want to be in love with my plates, by how the food is arranged, by how the sauce is brightened with herbs, by the way these glazed carrots and onions have been placed. We don't have the right to mistreat what we're making. Precision for me is respect for the dish.

If there's any one chef I learned this from it is Jean-Louis Palladin. I first met him when he came to my pastry shop. Who was this guy with the big eyes and glasses and this overflow of passion? We sat down and talked about food for hours. He invited me for his birthday, and we were best friends for twenty years. He was the guy who did cooking that was as we say in French, *au pif,* improvised but up to a point, never beyond where it could endanger the dish's soul. Everything he did used to look so fresh. A terrine at Jean-Louis was not some slab covered in fat. It was full of vegetables and fresh, and it looked as if the dawn had made it. If Jean-Louis was serving you a soup, it was pure green. He'd make the soup at the last second. It was not oxidized. He was a cook with his own style. You saw his food and you knew it could be nobody else. He supremely understood what it is to be a virtuoso; his technical mastery created the dish without imposing on it. It's hard to explain, but it's one of the mysteries of food.

I was cooking for an event in L.A. that he was supposed to cook at, and he called me from Las Vegas where he was working then and said, "Michel, I can't come. I'm very sick." I knew he was very sick because I'd asked him to go and see a doctor. He sent the food, and I took care of the food, and then he called a week later to say he had one year to live. The doctor told him he had cancer. He moved back with his wife to Washington, and when I opened Citronelle at the Latham, in Georgetown, I used to go and see him three or four times a week. Toward the end he was so weak he was not able to move one inch. *"Michel, donne-moi un coup de main,"* he'd say. He died November 25, 2001. I was happy he was not suffering anymore.

That changed me, and since then I try to spend more time with my kids. I try to appreciate things. Life is very short. The problem with being a chef is that you can often feel like a priest of your profession. You feel like there is nothing outside, and there's hardly any space for the rest of your life. You might feel like you're not working, but your children, your spouse, your partner, they do feel like you're working because you're not there. If Jean-Louis left a legacy I feel it is to be aware of that. We have chosen the hardest profession to find a balance in, but we must strive for that. Sometimes, when I'm leaving the restaurant an hour early to go home or when I'm taking a long morning walk, I sneak a glance at the sky. *"Tu vois, Jean-Louis,"* I say. "I'm learning, Jean-Louis, do you see?"

Alain Sailhac

Born in France, Alain Sailhac began his career at age fourteen as an apprentice at the Capion restaurant, in his hometown of Millau. Sailhac became the chef de cuisine at Le Mistral and Le Manoir in New York and executive chef at L'Hôtel Royal in New Caledonia and Le Perroquet in Chicago. Returning to New York, he became the executive chef at Le Cygne, which received its first-ever four-star rating from the *New York Times* during his tenure, and then went to Le Cirque. He received the Silver Toque when he was named Chef of the Year by Maîtres Cuisiniers de France. He is currently dean emeritus at The French Culinary Institute, where he brings nearly fifty-five years of experience to his students.

I started cooking professionally when I was fourteen and three months. The war was not over for that long; it was 1950. Everything was scarce; we didn't have meat because all the cattle had disappeared. We bought meat from Argentina, so everything was frozen. We received enormous pieces of frozen meat in the kitchen; we learned butchering on them. When you learn butchering you learn on the neck, where you have so many bones. If I left one scrap of meat, my chef would say, "Alain you didn't do a good job." You learned to use everything. You had to pay attention. Maybe if I started now it would be different. Here it's a country of bounty. They have a good excuse; they have plenty, plenty of everything. They don't realize carrots cost money, so they will take a little part from both sides and throw it away. You can and should use that for a stock.

We were six in the family. For us, respect for product started from want. I remember when I was a kid, eight, nine years old, going for bread, and the Germans took everything and I had to be in line thirty minutes. And the bread we received was black bread that came from Germany. When you opened it, it was totally green with mold. We never threw away the whole thing. My mother cleaned it up, cut around the mold, and we ate the rest—and we lived to tell.

My father took me to work in a restaurant when I was just over fourteen. There wasn't much of a discussion; that was going to be my job. For the first six months I was peeling the vegetables and washing the salad. I'd pick up the coal in the morning at seven o'clock and build the fire. Then I'd clean up and make sure that when the big chef came at nine o'clock everything would be hot and clean. One day he said to me, "Sailhac, you're going to do a different thing. We're going to have zucchini tonight and I am going to show you how to cook zucchini." He showed me. I cut the zucchini. I didn't peel it. And I fried it. I was fourteen years and eight months. I did the zucchini. It was crispy. It was delicious. On my day off, I made the zucchini for my mother. Suddenly, I wasn't sleeping at my tasks but felt as if I became alive. Something happened to me, and I understood that the transformation of food was something I wanted to do. I knew it happened, but I'd never done it myself.

When I became a professional, I started a career where I moved around a lot, not just between countries but places in a city. I never had my own restaurant but I got to have a lot of freedom. There was an organization called the Société Culinaire, in Paris, that essentially was like a clearinghouse for chef's jobs. You paid them about a hundred dollars a year, and they found you a job. I'd already worked in Greece and in a hotel in Guadeloupe when I went in and said I wanted to go to the U.S. I wanted to learn English. They found me a chef who was opening a restaurant in New York. He was Raymond Oliver, a very well-known food personality in France. I went to see him. He said, "You want to be a chef in the U.S.?" Yes. "You have your papers?" Yes. "When do you want to go? We need you on Monday." On Monday I arrived in the U.S.

I worked at Le Manoir and Le Mistral and I was sous-chef with André René at the Plaza. I left for two years and I went to work first in New Caledonia, then in Germany, and in Paris, too. Someone sent me a note asking if I wanted to be a chef in Chicago. Jovan Trboyevic was opening a place there. I was in Chicago for ten months. I came back to New York, I saw André Soltner. He said, "I have something interesting for you. Do you want to go to Le Cygne, because the chef is leaving?"

This is all a lot of place names, but what I understand now is that as important as developing a style, I was developing a system. Efficiency is a very important part of a successful restaurant. You cannot have huge labor costs and you cannot have customers waiting half an hour between courses, and it is in the person of the chef that those two requirements meet. At Le Cygne, I was doing practical cuisine. It was the beginning of nouvelle cuisine, and we did a lot of *à la minute* dishes. The kitchen was very small. We took care that there weren't too many people. Two people in the morning and two people at night: one pâtissier and one pantry man, and me working double shifts. That was it. We served seventy-five for lunch and one hundred and fifty at dinner. It was clear, neat, and very fast.

We cut out the cream, the flour, and the butter. We simplified. We learned, or relearned, I should say, that you didn't always need sauces. You can use the juice of the fish at the last moment. No stock. You cook at the last moment. That kind of cooking was very important for me. We were the first to get four stars from Mimi Sheraton. I didn't know what that meant because I didn't read the paper. But one day they came into the kitchen. "It's the *New York Times*. Okay, put on your toque, we're taking a picture." When the review came out, it was fantastic. I went on vacation just at that moment. I received so many offers that wanted to double and triple my salary. When I came back I said to the owner, "Look, if you double my salary, I'll stay." He said, "No problem, Alain." He doubled my salary. Two months after, he said, "Alain, now I have another chef. You can go anytime."

I was in France, back in my hometown of Millau, finishing the house I was going to retire in, when I received a call. "Hey, Alain, *tu travailles pas?*" It was my friend André Soltner. He just won't let me not work. "You want to work?" he asked. "Yes, I want to work." "Good, I have a friend who has a restaurant, and the chef is leaving. Would you be interested?" I said, "Your friends at Le Cygne were very nice but a little stingy, but I'm going to tell you what I want." When I told him, he said, "You are totally insane. You ask too much. I don't understand you." I said, "Hey, André, I don't have a restaurant. I'm a chef, so I have to make money." He called me two days later. "Sirio wants to meet you in Montecatini."

I drove my little Volkswagen to Italy. I was sitting in the restaurant where Sirio told me to go when I saw a guy open the door, and I said to my wife at that time, "Look, we have John Wayne." I saw John Wayne talk to the maître d', and John Wayne come to our table. He said, "I'm Sirio Maccioni." He even walked like John Wayne. We talked, and he offered me the job of chef at Le Cirque, and that was to be my adventure.

We'd had a lot of businesspeople at Le Cygne; at Le Cirque, we had businesspeople, too, but we also had the social crust. Big names, presidents, kings, queens. Frank Sinatra in the corner, the king of Spain somewhere with his family. The king's father, the count of Barcelona, had an apartment in the hotel above us. Sirio each time would say, "Alain, you have to say hello to the king." I'd change my apron—I was a working chef—and go out. I didn't know if I had to say, King Carlos, Juan Carlos, Monsieur the King, Monsieur le Roi. The second time he told me, "Look, call me Carlos." So I called him Carlos, and he called me Alain. He didn't call me Chef. He'd say, "Alain, I would like to have something very simple." And what I noticed in my little life of chef is the highest people, they are very simple.

Sirio was a great employer for a chef. Everyone who worked at Le Cirque had an opportunity to be noticed. He deserves the best because he gives the opportunity to the chef to use the best. All the time he would say, "Alain, buy the best." We had forty kilos of caviar in the icebox. It was really plush. In truffle season I had a guy come in the kitchen with a big basket. His name was Paul Urbani. His two sons are in New Jersey. He had a lot of truffles to sell. Three hundred dollars a pound, in 1978. I went to see Sirio. "How many pounds does he have?" Ten. "Buy everything." So we would shave the truffles at the last moment. The truffles were kept in a bowl with uncooked rice, and the waiter shaved them. Only white truffles, of course. Now chefs shave black truffles, too, but those have a more intense flavor when cooked. When someone had a big name, I had my little truffle slicer and I went out to do it. Sirio gave me a silver one. We were selling the truffles for fifty dollars a portion.

Cooking in a high-powered restaurant is a challenge every morning and every night. The cooks are very excited during the service; a lot of things are going on. You see all those plates, all those people being served, you have a lot of adrenaline. It's like running: after two or three miles you actually feel better than at the start. It's the same in kitchens: The beginning of a service can be rough. After that, you work and everybody works together. The chef has to control that, but control it in a very subtle way. You don't want to check on everybody, because if you check on everybody, you know what? People don't like it. You have to check without telling them that you're checking. You have to see. It's a very fine thing, very hard to define.

When a chef is in charge of a kitchen he has two rushes during the day, so he should keep his calm all the time, because if the chef is suddenly nervous he builds up tension instead of bringing calm. A kitchen is orchestrated chaos. The best chef in the world without a team is absolutely nothing, so a chef has to be not only someone who knows his trade but when you become chef, you become a father, a diplomat, a psychologist. You have to know your people. You have to know who is going to be good, less good, who can do such and such a task, who you can trust. You have to accept also that in a kitchen sometimes people cannot perform properly at that moment. You become a chef if you accept that.

Kitchens today are better than they used to be. The structure is entirely different. Chefs are very well educated, much more than before. Menus today are also more studied. You're going to have ten apps, ten main courses, and maybe one special. It's very professional. Chefs become more precise. When I was at Le Cirque, I had forty-five different entrées. It's very hard to be in a kitchen with forty-five entrées. We made seven specials. Half the customers wanted to order off the menu, and we had two and a half seatings every single night. So the kitchen has to be well organized. The first people who come at six o'clock, you have to serve them in one hour because you know very well you're going to be in trouble after that. You know very well that if people come at six they don't want to stay in your restaurant for two hours. And it's not in your interest, or the interest of anybody, that those people stay there. Otherwise it doesn't work. That belongs to the organization.

The way the menu was written and the way the kitchen was run was organized for speed. You had tools. We knew we were going to sell forty lobster salads, so we had those plated. We let the customers put on the vinaigrette. They loved that. The plat du jour is another tool. You can prepare roasts and braises, twenty or thirty portions that you know you're going to sell, and that makes things easier. We did bollito misto; it's like a pot-au-feu, Italian style. We served it in the kitchen in a pot, sent it out, and the waiter ladled it from the pot to the plate. Then they kept what was left on the table with the lid on. Then you can serve yourself. That's good. Bouillabaisse is a good plat du jour, too. You cook at the moment, but you have all the ingredients arranged in the dishes. From the oven to the table. Fantastic. A good waiter can help, too, because they can push things; but, you know, some people you can drive, but you can't drive a New Yorker. They know they want to eat something, and that's it.

What puts many cooks in a mess today is they want to cook from scratch at the last moment. You need the staff to do *à la minute*. You need trained cooks; you have to train them. You need people who can move. When I say moving, I don't mean just the individual at their station but the kitchen as a team. Whoever is expediting has to move, too. They are the conductor of the orchestra. You have some people who will wait five minutes before they will fire a table so the cooks start preparing the food. Five minutes on this order, five minutes for the next order, and then ten minutes for the next one. That's why speed is so important. Move now! It can't wait. In a kitchen everything has to be focused on the service. You cannot start to do your sliced leeks for the soup for tomorrow. No, service is service. Everybody is functioning and focused on the service and on the customer.

The *mise en place* has to be done before, not during, the service. I suppose in a restaurant with only a few tables you can do it. But I was lucky; all the restaurants I worked at were busy all the time. Most of the time, the problem that you have in the kitchen is the stress. The saucier has two feet in front of him and two feet in the back, and he has to handle so many things. If you're not organized, creativity is not going to come out.

There is a huge satisfaction in being able to say, "We just served three hundred people, and we did a good job." At the end of the service you have an unbelievable satisfaction, and you are entirely released. Service to me is like fighting a war, like winning a war. You win the war every single lunch or every single dinner. If you have too many complaints, you know very well that you lost the war. And at that moment you have to rethink. Sometimes you mess up even if you're organized. Rib of beef for two and the guy asks for it rare, and it's medium rare. I want to tell you, you have to start again. That's thirty minutes. So even if two people complain, you've lost.

When I was at Le Cirque, it was an unbelievable challenge that I met every single day for eight and a half years of my life. And I am very proud of that. I've seen the Secret Service follow a dish of mine all along a corridor so nothing could be thrown into it before it was placed in front of the president of the United States. For a boy from Millau, that's not bad. And yet the greatest satisfaction of my career has come during the last fifteen years of my life. I feel extraordinarily pleased to be dean of studies at The French Culinary Institute and to see the people come with their passion to this school. I share that with them, and am lucky to be with them. I learn from everybody. Their first day here they don't even know what a chef's knife is. And when they graduate they have a path. I know what finding that feels like. It's wonderful to be among people who come with their passion and to be able to give them the tools to have that passion fulfilled.

Arun
Sampanthavivat

Arun Sampanthavivat was born and raised in a southern province of Thailand. After living in Germany and Japan for his academic studies, he came to Chicago to work on his doctorate, and eventually opened a restaurant there. Despite no formal training as a chef, Arun's Restaurant has received much praise for its sophisticated Thai cuisine. Sampanthavivat has received several awards, including Best Chef Midwest by the James Beard Foundation.

In Thailand, before we say good morning we say, "Have you eaten yet?" Snacks are mostly noodles. There are lots of dishes with everything in one bowl, like rice topped with curry.

Little fried dishes tend to be appetizers. A typical Thai restaurant in Thailand serves hot-and-sour soup, a couple of different types of noodles, and some spicy salads like papaya salad. Desserts aren't usually served in a Thai restaurant. You go for a walk and you find your dessert. By the time you reach dessert you're full, so dessert is not much of a focus in Thai cuisine. You always eat with people. The sense of participation, of a sort of gathering, is an important component. It starts when we go to temple and share food. We always share the experience

203

of being together and eating. When I was young, at eleven o'clock at night there would be a cart with egg noodles going around. Everybody in the neighborhood would run out with a plate and chopsticks and they would stand there eating and talking with the neighbors.

I grew up in the southern part of Thailand, on a rubber plantation. We lived in a small town, and the plantation was run by other people. We were like the landlords. I was very lucky. My grandfather was Chinese; my grandmother was pure Thai. So I learned two different cuisines from them. They never ate the same cuisine, and never ate together. My grandmother would eat only Thai food, and my grandfather only ate Chinese food. I would eat with both of them. They lived very well together, but they ate separately.

It was a bit like a feast every day. We would have eight to ten types of food on the table. Most Thais learn to cook well because they always have to take food to temple. This is the most important thing in daily life for Thai people, so they try to make their best. When they bring food to the temple everyone is somewhat competing to see who can do better, even the same curry. You bring the monks food every day, but when there is an important religious day, you bring a big feast.

My grandfather was very knowledgeable about Chinese cooking. At the table he always directed me and gave me instruction about what is good for you to be healthy, and went as far as to get very unusual ingredients from Singapore and Malaysia. If I didn't pay attention he would knock me on the head with chopsticks. "You have to learn, you have to learn all of this," he would say.

My grandmother taught me how to make curry. She would pound it in the mortar and pestle while I recited poetry to her. In Thailand they say, men want to hear the sound a woman makes with a mortar and pestle before they get married. It's usually made of stone and is probably the most important tool in Thai cooking. Almost every Thai household, at least traditionally, couldn't be without one. Thai curry doesn't come from powder but from many ingredients pounded into a smooth paste. Nowadays you can use an electric blender, but for me the curry becomes watery and changes the whole format of the curry. You can also make dips in it and you can make medicines when you grind herbs. A mortar and pestle gives you control that no machine can. You have to use the wrist of your hand. Then you grind and crush.

There are certain formulas that have been proven for centuries. With this you can do that. So you cannot stretch your imagination too far if you do not know the basics. You have to know the classic principles. You learn the basic formula first. If you screw up the paste you still have some room left to adjust, because the last process is seasoning. How you balance this saltiness, this sourness, and this sweetness together; you do that in the last minute. That's why Thai cooking is based on taste and trial. You do not go blindly with the recipe. Because if you do so, not only would you miss all the fun, but then it's not really done to your taste. Recipes only can give you the guidance, the more-or-less, but that more-or-less varies from one person to the other.

The basic herbs for Thai curry are lemongrass, Thai ginger or galangal, garlic, shallot, chili pepper, dry or fresh, depending on what kind of curry. Sometimes you have turmeric. Another part that's important is dried shrimp, or you can add cilantro later on. That's the basic of a Thai curry, whether it's green or red. If it's green that means you don't use the red chili, rather fresh green chili. But in a red curry you use red dry chili. Certain things you don't pound, such as basil. You pound plants or herbs that have fiber, but you do not pound leafy things; even kefir lime leaves that have strong leaves. And you don't usually cook too long. Very quick cooking and out. That's why stir-frying is the best process for cooking basil. Sometime you eat it raw.

I learned this from my grandmother. She couldn't read very well but she had a good memory. So when I was a young child I would sit by her and read for her, and she would listen and recite back. It was a ritual. I was learning story upon story, even fairy tales. While I was reading I couldn't watch her make the curry, but while she was reciting I could. She never stopped pounding.

My father believed strongly in education, because it's the only way in which you can survive in Thailand. You have to strive to have the highest education possible to guarantee your future. So when I was ten I was sent to school in Bangkok. I got into the best high school and eventually into the best school of arts, which was founded in 1868 and trained students to serve the king. So it was a privileged and elite group. I was from nowhere, from the countryside. I set up my goal around eleven years of age. I wanted to study literature because I loved poetry. I said to myself, "I have got to go in this direction," without knowing that was the hardest road ahead.

In university, I specialized in Thai literature and poetry, and my minor subject was German. I chose German because everyone chose to study French. I wanted to be among the few. I did well, and after I graduated I went to Germany and I hoped to get into the university in

Hamburg. At that time there was an energy crisis, and I couldn't find a job. I was offered a job in Tokyo instead, to help write a documentary film. While there I got accepted at Sofia International University, once again the elite school in Japan, the international school for Asia. I don't know how I got in, but I did. I graduated with a master's degree in international relations. My professors suggested I should go and get a Ph.D. in America and go to Chicago for theory, which I was interested in. I knew one day I was going to have to work but I didn't want to think about it. I had no idea about what kind of work I would do.

I was accepted to the University of Chicago, and then, at the brink of getting my Ph.D., something happened. A group of Thai people that I knew in Hyde Park near campus wanted to open a small Thai restaurant and asked me to help. I told them I could loan them some money but they had to open a fine-dining type Thai restaurant because I had not seen that here before. This is one thing we have to realize. Most Thai restaurants here are not a good representation of real Thai food. Most storefront restaurants do a simple kind of cooking, quick-cooking, stir-frying, close to Chinese. They accepted that, but then before the restaurant opened they all chickened out. I was left on my own.

I had never done anything with a restaurant. No cooking, no serving—zero. I convinced myself that I had nothing to lose and I should accept the challenge. That was the moment of no return, because I had never worked in a Thai restaurant and I wasn't going to try to duplicate one. Everything was quite original and unique. I hired a few people but had to do most things myself. The way I conceived my first menu was perhaps not a rational approach; in fact it was quite an irrational approach to food: I sketched all the pictures of the dishes first. By painting the dishes, I saw how the ingredients would be combined together.

I started with two different kinds of menu. One would be called the daily menu, which listed no more than twenty items. The other menu would be six to eight items, what I called the rotating menu. So I had two kinds of menus right from the beginning, so it was very exciting for people to see. Two months after I opened, I was noticed by the *Chicago Tribune*. I got three stars right away. Then I got three and a half stars from the *Sun-Times*. I was pleased but also amazed, since I didn't have formal training or proper ingredients so to speak.

You had to be very resourceful. At that time you didn't buy lemongrass, not to even mention kefir lime. You tried to make do with whatever you could; even the dry kefir lime was precious. Then you tried to reconcile. I would not hesitate to go with ingredients that weren't Thai. You tried to incorporate those. For example, you could use Italian basil. You sacrificed a little bit of the flavor but you could still maintain the integrity of Thai cooking. You didn't even have the Chinese broccoli, so we had to use American broccoli. Then, as Laotian and Vietnamese refugees started arriving in Chicago, we were able to piggyback on their ingredients. We also used a lot of Mexican ingredients—like cilantro, for example; we used jalapeño instead of Thai chili. For me it was very important to find something close enough to the idea of what I actually had. So we didn't have fresh lemongrass; well, I'd much rather use dry lemongrass than use ready-made chili paste that comes in a can that has a disgusting, preservative kind of aroma.

I think part of the reason for our success is that we never tried to

simplify Thai cooking for the sake of the American customer. That is something that ethnic restaurants always tried to do. For example, though we didn't serve strictly regional food, we didn't pretend that regions didn't exist. There are four regions in Thailand. The northern part of Thailand is adjacent to Burma, so the cooking has that influence from Burmese cooking. The Burmese themselves got influenced by the Indians. I was in Burma once and tried their curry; it's quite different from Thai curry and not spicy at all. When it comes into Thai cuisine, then, it becomes like a new interpretation—and once it got into my hands, yet another interpretation. The north is not close to the sea, so a lot of dishes are based on meat, particularly pork. And the flavor itself is richer than you would find in the rest of the country.

When you get to the northeast part of Thailand, which is close to

Laos, you have a lot of nice spicy salad type of cooking, with lots of herbs. In that part of the country people eat very little food because it's a scarce resource. So they can go to the rice fields with a little sticky rice and a bit of chili dip that could last them the whole day. (A little chili dip so they can eat as hot as they want with a little vegetables and herbs, or maybe dry fish.) But now everywhere in Thailand is rich, and you can find anything.

Bangkok has the most elegant Thai food, mainly focused on presentation. Royal cuisine is meticulous, with lots of carving and wrapping of the food and rolling into bite-size portions. Southern cooking is salty and spicy, and influenced by Singapore, Malaysia, Indonesia, and China. In southern Thai cooking, we eat lots of curried seafood. That part of the country has lots of coconut trees, so cooking from that area uses a lot of coconut milk, particularly in all kinds of curry. It's very intense. I love it because it's quite refreshing, too.

So we had to educate the American customer. When they came to the restaurant, we felt we should guide them. A chili sauce won't necessarily work with everything. That's why there are hundreds of chili sauces. In a curry, every single herb has not only its own property, flavor, and characteristic, but they work collectively, as a group, when put together right.

We also continued to learn at the restaurant. In menu writing you have both East and West. The Eastern part is that you serve it family-style, sticking classically to your principles of cooking. You certainly can't eat curry alone, as you have to have something else to help reinforce or enhance it. But in the appetizer, you can serve one at a time. Serving something individually is Western, not Thai. Technically, in

Thai cooking, you have a big wok station. I also use a lot of oven roasting because I find it yields better texture and form. I also use ingredients that are not indigenous to Thai cooking. For example, with something like arugula, which is not known in Thai cooking, I could use that, just as I might use salmon. This is Western influence, but approached within the parameters of Thai cooking, not of fusion food. I think it is a bit like poetry. When I write poetry in Thai, I see things the Thai way; if I write in English, it's very philosophical.

The success of my restaurant has allowed me to contribute to many interesting things, such as the Taste of Thailand Festival in Chicago. But it has also allowed me to return to my roots. Most Thai men are supposed to become monks when they're eighteen years of age, and I made a vow that one day I would do so. I was very late. Some time ago my mother fell ill, and I said if she survives this I would become a monk. So right after I did a Taste of Thailand Festival in Chicago I decided to become a monk. I went to the temple where the king was ordained. The ceremony is very rigid; you have to be able to recite a long text. I passed that, then took off to Chiang Mai, up north, and stayed in a temple completely isolated on a mountain.

I had to climb five hundred and eighteen steps to get to the top of the mountain, and I had to go up and down six times a day. I had to get up at three o'clock to do meditation and chant sitting on a cold stone floor. Then I'd come down about five o'clock to beg for food in the village, which was about two and a half kilometers from the temple. Begging for food makes you so humble. When you go to a house and a little boy offers you a handful of sticky rice, and he has to get up just to offer that, it makes you appreciate every act. Then you bring the food up to the temple, and all the monks dine together. They serve the patriarch first, and by the time the food came to me there was almost nothing left. But even though we only ate once a day, during that time I was not hungry at all. The whole day would pass with meditation, learning, and discipline.

Later in the afternoon you sweep the temple floors and all those steps and walk back again. They shave your head. It's the tradition that once you become a monk you will want nothing of these worldly things. You will be rid of all the desires. We believe as Buddhists that one day through this we will be able to go to the right path of the Buddha. We will be rid of human desires and be able to conquer whatever suffering that we have. You try to reach that point, but that's the most difficult thing to do. To follow the Buddha like that you have to already have lived thousands upon thousands of lives, and each life you have to perfect. That's almost impossible. But you can keep doing good things consciously and mindfully. You feel very pure inside and have that good concentration. You know that you're a good person; you know that you are decent.

I stayed there for fifteen days. If I had stayed one day longer it would enter the rainy season and that would mean I could not get out of the temple for three months. I couldn't afford to do that. The experience has made me become more at peace and look at things with acceptance. I am less hot tempered than I was before, much more patient and mindful of what I do. Meditation is good for everyone; it's like you have water in a glass with a lot of impurities, but once you sit it there, all the impurities sink to the bottom. When you cook food you have to concentrate. Focus. And if you have that meditation skill, it helps you a lot. Step by step, almost automatically, you kind of structure what you're going to do. That's one benefit. But a greater benefit is that with your cooking you feel that it is a gift that you are giving. So you want to cook right. You pay as much attention as you can and you create a habit of doing things with care.

Marcus Samuelsson

Marcus Samuelsson was born in Ethiopia and adopted by a Swedish couple. After graduation from the culinary institute in Götenberg, he worked in Switzerland and Austria, where he learned to craft fine pastry. He began his career at Aquavit, in New York, and later spent time in France studying under Georges Blanc. He eventually became executive chef and part owner of Aquavit, where he quickly garnered three stars from the *New York Times*. He is also the culinary director at Riingo. Early in his career, Samuelsson received the James Beard Foundation Award for Rising Star Chef and later received Best Chef New York City. The Culinary Institute of America has recognized him as one of the "Great Chefs of America."

Every Thursday people in Sweden eat yellow split pea soup. The tradition goes back hundreds of years. You take them out on Tuesday, you soak them, you cook the soup on Wednesday, and Thursday you eat it. The next day you can make pancakes from what's left. Every day has its dish. You have your herrings on Tuesday and you have your pea soup on Thursday and your beef patty on Friday. You're basically saving up to get the roast on Sunday. When an

215

entire country understands that, you're dealing with a very homogenized culture. It's largely Protestant, and people tend to stay in their regions. Up until recently it was also a poor man's culture. I was two and a half years old when I moved to Sweden from Ethiopia. My biological mother died of tuberculosis, so I was in an orphanage until I was adopted. I don't have memories of Ethiopian cooking. I grew up in a Swedish family knowing you eat split pea soup on Thursdays. I grew up as a Swede.

My parents have very interesting backgrounds. My mother comes from an extremely poor family in Sweden, and she has that mentality still today. You don't throw anything away. You eat chicken one day and chicken soup the next day and then, if you can make chicken dumplings, the third day that's what you do, regardless of how much money you have. My grandfather never liked butter because he was used to eating the grease in the pan. He could never eat anything else but boiled potatoes. If we had pasta, he had a side of boiled potatoes, too. As a child that was something I just didn't understand. His generation had a very rough background; they started work when they were ten or eleven.

My father's family always owned their own business. He was a geologist. He had his own company, and they did very well. The liberal in him decided that since they couldn't have kids, they would adopt; so they did. I have two sisters, one is Ethiopian biological, like me, one is Jamaican-Swedish. My parents were white; our cousins are Korean. The whole family looks so different. So my mother basically raised us as rock stars. "Okay, we're going out to the store now. People are going to be staring at you. So be aware and just be fabulous, just be better." People touched our hair, people wanted to check our skin, kids started to cry—all these things happened because they'd never seen people of color.

I started cooking with my grandmother, my mother's mother. She was a really good cook. She'd been a maid, and she cooked a lot for the family she worked for. I became aware of taste because of her. I realized that time and taste go together. You have to put time in to make it taste good. Because you could have meatballs or you could have *her* meatballs. By age ten I knew what was homemade—even if it was in her style. She boiled the hell out of beans. For her, fish meant cured fish. It was still very bare back then. We didn't have fresh vegetables or herbs. We had root vegetables like celeriac and beets; we had great apples and plums in early fall. Our desserts were all berry based, or rhubarb. The central culinary philosophy was all about hoarding. You pickled or preserved things because you didn't know when you'd have it again. I have early memories of going mushroom hunting with my grandmother. She'd make a warm chanterelle sandwich, pretty fantastic, but not to be repeated. The next day she either pickled or froze them all because you never know what's going to happen.

Being raised in a small country has lots of advantages. Our reference points are Japan, Russia, England, *and* America. It's not just America. Things aren't viewed only from one point of view. You have to learn German, French, *and* English. At the time I was growing up, the big fear was that Russia would come and invade us. That could happen at any given time, as it was the cold war. If America came, that meant more TV, which would be okay. But if Russia came, we'd be shut off. Those were the type of things you thought about because that's what your parents were talking about.

I traveled with my dad all over Europe. Wherever they needed to build a bridge or find any kind of minerals, his company was called and he took us with him. From a very early age we had to eat local food in these places. So when you go to a place like Communist Prague in 1982, it's different than going to Prague with its beautiful bars today. There are even vegetables today. At the same time, my dad was giving me lessons in how to deal with life. Racism is a universal beast and it exists in all cultures. It's not just a white phenomenon. It's everywhere. My dad said to me, "Okay, Marcus, you know you can't fight. You can't fight because you're going to be in a lot of fights. It just doesn't work. You have to communicate in a different way." That's kind of hard when you're fourteen, fifteen, and you want to fight every day, but I understood the wisdom of it even then.

I was a better athlete than student. Still today, I view myself as a failed soccer player. The whole athlete experience was great when I started to study cooking because there is a link there. Some type of teamwork is involved, and you can't be a complete ass, because if you're not a nice person in the kitchen you're not going to get the help you need. It's the same in soccer: if you're not a good guy, you're just not going to get the ball. You work hard at both. A long day is not a big deal. You can stand for however many hours and you can outwork people. There is something competitive in cooking. Not that you have to compete, but you have to do something very well, you have to be noticed without being the loudest, and you have to take pride in what you do. I happen to like that. If you don't like it, then the kitchen is not for you. Maybe being in a band is for you. Or being something else. For me, if I worked hard I got a scholarship. At the end of the day there was a carrot somewhere. "Marcus," someone would say, "I'm sending you to France." I just knew early that if you work hard there is somebody, somewhere, watching.

My first experience outside Sweden was in Switzerland, at the Victoria-Jungfrau Hotel, in Interlaken. It was a great place, and I was there for two and a half years. Students from all over the world came to this place to learn how to serve people. Whether it was the kitchen, back of the house, or front of the house, at a very high standard. There was a brigade. I had never seen this French-organized kitchen before. And there I was a commis. We started in the garden; we had to learn about the herbs. Three months later you were in the butchering and then you were in the garde manger. So it was this rigid system before you got on the line, which was probably eighteen months.

People cracked left and right, and new people came in. Although there was a lot of failure in this whole experience, I just knew these guys are going for it. I met fifty-year-old chef sauciers, a forty-five-year-old chef *entremetier*. This was their life. These are not celebrity chefs; these are cooks that worked the station for thirty-five years.

We had to call each other by our surnames. We were eighteen, nineteen years old, and I wasn't allowed to call my best friend Hans Peter by his first name. In the kitchen I would have to say, *"Herr Dorff, Entschuldigung* [excuse me]...," to a nineteen-year-old. You didn't address yourself to the chef at all. The chef could line us up, and we had to make a perfect omelet when we were in the middle of stuff. "Okay, Mr. Samuelsson," you'd hear, and you had to do something. For him, a perfect omelet was a hot pan but no color. If you browned the omelet you could get fired. But it wasn't mean; it was just old school in every sense of the word. Sometimes it would be "Okay, Mr. Samuelsson, now you're going to Gstaad." I had to go and help out in a different town. We're not that busy, so we'll send our guys away. It's old school; it's beautiful.

219

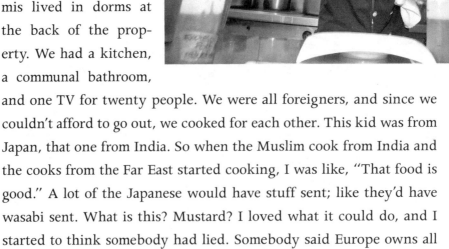

On a parallel track with this classic kitchen I was learning about other food. The commis lived in dorms at the back of the property. We had a kitchen, a communal bathroom, and one TV for twenty people. We were all foreigners, and since we couldn't afford to go out, we cooked for each other. This kid was from Japan, that one from India. So when the Muslim cook from India and the cooks from the Far East started cooking, I was like, "That food is good." A lot of the Japanese would have stuff sent; like they'd have wasabi sent. What is this? Mustard? I loved what it could do, and I started to think somebody had lied. Somebody said Europe owns all the good food, and that was a lie. So even while I was in the heart of it I knew I had to get out.

The process would take some time. I would go to Austria to learn about strudel and Kaiserschmarrn and the delicacy of serving a perfect glass of water with coffee. For me, learning pastry was indispensable. I believe you create a meal like my grandmother created meals, from chicken soup to chicken dumplings to gingersnaps, so it was all her food. In a restaurant it shouldn't be those are pastry people and these are garde manger people—it's all our food. At Georges Blanc, I became the only person who could translate for the Japanese. So right away I was useful. I also learned how you start asking questions. You don't get paid in these jobs, but you learn how to do the most classical and best dishes again and again and then you start to ask yourself questions: What do I like about this? How will I use it?

In between there were trips back to Switzerland when my mom and I would spend hours in the local library trying to find grants that would allow me to continue studying. When I felt I knew something, I started working for a cruise line. We traveled all over the world, and I saw great food that had nothing to do with Europe. I saw Mexican food that was not Tex-Mex. I saw the stuff that happened in Marrakech and Fez, and I saw the fish market in Bangkok and the Tokyo fish market, and I saw Hong Kong. All these places changed my life completely, and I said, "Okay, now I get it."

I knew I wasn't going to exclude this part of the world in my cooking. I wasn't focused on whether it was Bangkok or Tokyo. I just knew, here is my background, why can't I take perfect turbot, steam it with lime leaves, and squeeze lemon or lime on it, and serve it with rice? No cream, butter, and it's ready. At the same time I was hearing about all these crazy chefs in America. I read something about Charlie Palmer. I read things about David Burke and Alfred Portale and Patrick Clark. They cooked French food, but it was New York French. Heirloom tomatoes with bass, pesto made with arugula. It was that simple. I started seeing *Food Arts* and magazines featuring bouillons instead of sauces, and I said, "Alright, I've got to go there."

In New York I saw for the first time a mixed clientele go into restaurants. It wasn't either Japanese tourists or European travelers or very wealthy Americans. In Europe those were the only people you served. Here there were young couples going out, women's lunches. Customers might be Indian or Chinese or black. It was not a homogenized pool of customers. I think that openness helped me a lot when I became chef at Aquavit at the age of twenty-four. I had to start writing menus. It was the first time I felt the pressure and responsibility that everything had to come from me.

In a very roundabout way Swedish cooking was conducive to creativity. Sweden has borrowed from both neighbors and trading partners. Germany, Greece, Turkey, are strong influences on Swedish cooking, as are the spices of Southeast Asia. In a traditional Swedish recipe like gingersnaps, you find ginger, cinnamon, and cardamom, things that obviously didn't grow in Sweden. So that was something like a first layer. Then I had our natural resources. Sweden is a country of lakes, rivers, and cold and clear salt waters, so we have fantastic seafood. Then there's an aesthetic layer, a very minimalist approach in presentation, which I've always loved. We even have the sugar layer. Because we traditionally salted to preserve foods, we devised something called one-two-three vinegar, which is one part vinegar, two parts sugar, and three parts water. That taste is what Swedish food is. It's sour and it's sweet.

So I work with these building blocks in any dish we do. I also think of textures, temperatures, and above all that it's flavor-driven food today, moving away from technique-driven food. For me to get a person who doesn't know anything about Sweden—never been to the country—to enjoy a Swedish dish compared to a Vietnamese dish, I have to think flavors and aesthetic, and I have to present it in an interesting way.

We do a lobster roll where we slice apples or Asian pear. We pickle them in one-two-three vinegar, then we make a lobster salad and roll it up like a sushi roll. We serve it very minimally on the plate with just a swirl of a sauce, such as horseradish sabayon. It's pretty precise in terms of how it's rolled; it leaves room on the plate for positive and negative space, which I think is important, and it has nice textures. The Asian pear is like a melon. That means the lobster can be very spicy because you have something that feeds off from that. Perfectly sliced gravlax can be a perfect dish, too. I sometimes do it with Tasmanian trout cured with a little bit of chilies, and though it's not strictly Swedish, it also kind of is. An aesthetic approach has become a way of identification.

New York allows you to be whatever five cultures you are and a New Yorker at the same time. So it's not surprising that I became aware of Ethiopia as a big part of me in New York. I'd go to restaurants and I'd just smell things that fascinated me, and then when I actually went to Ethiopia I'd be in this constant state of fitting in but not fitting in: you look like them but you can't speak like them. Gradually I became fascinated by Africa, not just as a person but also as a cook.

You can do a tour of the continent in staple foods alone. Senegal has a rich rice culture, which eventually found its way to North Carolina through the slave trade. Ghana uses fermented corn. In Nigeria and Cameroon they use casaba mash, and in South Africa they have polenta. Ethiopia is slightly different in that it has never been colonized, and the wheat for the *Njera* bread, which is like a sourdough pancake, could only be grown in the Ethiopian highlands. South African food has Cape Malay food, which is fantastic. You find Indian Chinese food in Africa tasting incredible. When you're in Mozambique and you find this Portuguese food that's the same as in Lisbon, and the same as in Bahia, in Brazil, to me that's just intriguing. I have never thought that the ultimate goal for food is to be discovered in the West. Vietnamese food was just as good when we didn't know about it here. But for the curious individual, Africa is just ready to be tapped into.

Chefs today are slash. We're slash everything. We are cooks. We have to be PR savvy. We have to be managers of finance. We have to do television. We have to do books. And you could say, "No, you don't." But you really have to. You have to be out there and do things in order for people to come to your restaurant. And our customers are changing. The symbol of the modern customer is the iPod. You don't listen to a whole album, you listen to one song. It can be hip-hop, rock, and Bob Marley in the same five-minute experience. That's how we like to eat, too. You need to eat in five minutes, you need to have a two-hour meal, and I now need to have a chicken dish for your friend who arrived an hour late. We are a business where we have to supply what people want, and at the same time stand for something. I think we can do it and come across with our Scandinavian point of view, but that balance is always hard.

And I wouldn't say we chefs make it easier on ourselves. You always feel guilty when you don't work, really guilty if you're not working on a Saturday night. I've never had three weeks' vacation in my life—and I come from Europe, where there's eight weeks' vacation. Just shutting off your phone and making sure that nobody can get to you is a major thing. So it's very hard for a chef to find balance in life outside work. It's not the industry; it's you yourself who has to do that. There are lots of great and passionate people in this industry, but I think it's something that you're raised with through work. You're in the business to serve and take pleasure in serving and take pride in saying, this is what we're about. So we can end up neglecting ourselves.

But as modern chefs we also have voices, and we have listeners on the other side. That is a great privilege, and it has allowed me, for example, to do voluntary work for UNICEF. You work with different opportunities that come your way and you create opportunities. And every year we can go back with a check. It doesn't have to go toward Ethiopia; that's not my focus. My biological mother died of tuberculosis; today it costs a dollar to save somebody from tuberculosis. One dollar. You think about that. If I have a voice, then talking about things like that is one of the things I feel I have to say. Working with UNICEF has also allowed me to visit orphanages. You go into an orphanage, and there are two thousand kids and they're all running toward you. And it's the best reality check you can ever have. It can be very emotional. You figure out, okay, how did I get picked out of this whole group? And how did I survive and start my journey? How did I go from here to learning about split pea soup?

André **Soltner**

André Soltner was born in Alsace and started his career at the age of fifteen with an apprenticeship at Hôtel du Parc in Mulhouse. After positions at the Royale Hôtel in Deauville, the Palace Hôtel in Switzerland, and Hôtel de l'Europe in Alsace, he became the head chef at the Parisian restaurant Chez Hansi. He eventually moved to the United States and for thirty-four years was the chef-owner of Lutèce, which was given a four-star rating by the *New York Times*. Soltner has received dozens of distinctions, including the French government's Légion d'Honneur and the James Beard Foundation Lifetime Achievement Award. He is currently the dean of classic studies at The French Culinary Institute.

I grew up in Alsace. It's the nicest part of the world. In terms of food, it's French food with a little plus. Of course, just after the war we had nothing. Every evening we had potatoes and onion *jus*. You roasted onions in a skillet until they were not just golden but brown, and put some flour in and some water and maybe some white wine. You cooked it and then you strained it like when you put warm milk in coffee and you don't want the skin. There was no meat in it but it was brown, so you could fool yourself. I hated it—and we ate it every day for two years.

My father was a cabinetmaker. A lot of his time was spent searching for food. He would barter. If a butcher needed a new cabinet, my father took some of the payment in meat. One of his great pleasures was wine. Whenever my father sold a cabinet, he got a barrel. He'd say, "Bring me a jar of sylvaner," and I would go down to the cellar. I'd take a little bit for myself and then I'd go upstairs. We always had about five barrels in the cellar. There is a hill in Thann, my hometown, called Rangen. It is one of the best vineyards in Alsace. It's granite stone. I had a Rangen from Zind Humbrecht on my wine list at Lutèce. Humbrecht is from Turkheim, so he wrote me a letter and asked me, as an Alsatian, to help him to come to America, and of course, as an Alsatian, I did.

My brother decided to be a cabinetmaker, and my mother said she didn't want two cabinetmakers in the family so I would be a cook. I first got an apprenticeship in Colmar, but they would literally beat you there. After two weeks I packed my suitcase and I went home and told my parents it was too tough. My parents then found a place for me in the Hôtel du Parc in Mulhouse, about twenty miles from my hometown. On the day my father signed the apprenticeship papers, the chef said, "Now he's mine." I adored my chef and wanted to be like him. His name was René Simon. I only realized later what a fine chef he was. He came from the generation that never really got recognized. We had to be there before him in the morning and we couldn't take off our aprons before him at night. He cared about us. We were his boys. He might slap you, but afterward he was sorry. I loved it there. On my day off I would cycle the twenty kilometers home with my dirty cooking vests on the back of the bike for my mother to wash, but I couldn't wait to get back to work.

The chef took our apprenticeships very seriously. Three months in each station and then we'd move on to the next. Once I was on pastry and I had to do vol-au-vents. I made the puff pastry and then I put them in the oven. This was a coal-burning oven; very hard to regulate the temperature for baking. He looked in and saw they were rising and he turned to the whole kitchen: "Look, Bubby's—they called me Bubby—his vol-au-vents are rising." I was so proud.

In those days there were traveling salesmen who went from town to town and restaurant to restaurant selling chef's knives and vests. One morning, about two months into my apprenticeship, a salesman came into our kitchen and put his suitcases up on a table. We all went over. My chef said it was time for me to get my own knives. This was a big deal. Every chef had his own knives. I remember I was worried that they would ask my father to pay for them, but it wasn't enough to stop me. On that morning I got a boning knife, a chef's knife, and a paring knife, and I felt I was on my way to becoming a chef. This was in 1948.

I was twenty-one when I went to Paris. I thought I was a good chef. I'd worked in a very elegant hotel in Deauville and also in Switzerland. But I wasn't ready for the speed that everyone worked at. Our chefs had made us wear big shoes, but in the kitchens in Paris everyone was wearing espadrilles and running around. I said to myself, "How can I be that fast?" Two days later I bought espadrilles. Even when I owned Lutèce everyone wore espadrilles. If the floor got wet, the water went through a little bit. On the other hand, if you dropped oil on your foot you could rip the espadrille off. In those days, I brought so many espadrilles over from France I could have opened a store.

I met André Surmain when he came to eat at Chez Hansi, an Alsatian brasserie in Montparnasse where I was working. He was doing lots of things in New York. He ran a cooking school with James Beard and he also catered for airlines. But he wanted to open a restaurant. Years earlier I used to play table tennis with a pastry chef who now did work for Surmain, and he told him he should meet me when he came to Paris. So he came to eat at Chez Hansi, and afterward I went to see him and he said how much he'd enjoyed the meal. Then he looked around and he said, "Can I speak to you?" I knew what that meant. That's the way you steal a chef.

So I came to New York in 1961. I found the quality of the ingredients depressing. Veal, mushrooms—everything looked tired. Still, I applied myself and pretty soon we got a nice review from Craig Claiborne. One star. I was very happy. I couldn't read English, but there was a picture of Lutèce. We had the most expensive restaurant in the U.S. Lunch was $8.50 and there was such a scandal, we had to go down to $6.50. We never did a hundred covers. I didn't lose money because I didn't have any money in it, but we weren't making much. After two years I said I wanted to go back to France but Surmain made me a thirty percent partner and I stayed, and eventually he sold it to me outright.

Well, I knew how to cook but I literally knew nothing about money. I had none. My accountant said to me, "You're going to close if you don't get cash flow." Cash flow? I didn't understand. I thought that as long as every day you made a little more than you spent you were okay. But it doesn't work that way. Thankfully, in those days

finances were somewhat simpler. We were on Fiftieth Street; Bankers Trust was on Fifty-second. One day I walked in with my chef's coat on. The teller asked me what I wanted, and I said, "I don't know, money." My English was still not too good. He looked at me and then told me to go into an office. I went in and the gentleman said, "What can I do for you?" I said, "Well, I have a restaurant but I need money." He asked me how much. "I don't know," I said. "Maybe with forty thousand I can do it." I signed the papers right there. I was very loyal to Bankers Trust after that, but that manager, I saw him for about a year and then he disappeared. I would have liked to be able to thank him when things took off.

In 1972 our clientele started to be everybody at the top of the professional and social world. They liked that we didn't have airs. My wife, Simone, greeted people at the door, and on their way to their table they could look into the open kitchen and say hi to me. It's very difficult when you work in a restaurant with your spouse. You have to set up in the beginning what's what. Simone never came to the kitchen. If there was a problem with something, she didn't tell the chef; she told me. On the other hand, if there was a problem with a customer and she detected even the slightest hint of rudeness, she looked straight past them.

When Jacqueline Kennedy came back to New York she asked me to do her party at her apartment, and that established us completely. I don't say this to be arrogant, but we were the absolute top restaurant in New York. President Nixon loved my cooking and he loved Alsatian wines. Once he came as someone else's guest. I went out to the dining room and asked the host what he'd like to eat. "Oh, ask the president," he said. He was very excited that he had the president as a guest. So I said, "Mr. President, what would you like to eat?" And he said, "The usual, André. Just make what you like." He was a real gentleman.

We were near the UN, and we had lots of ambassadors. One of them didn't honor his reservation on two separate occasions. We used to keep the tables, just in case they were late. So the second time he didn't show up, I called the embassy. Ambassadors don't pick up the phone, so I said to the person, "This is André Soltner of restaurant Lutèce. Tell His Excellency that I will never cook for him again." This was in the morning. We used to keep the door locked and the deliverymen would ring the bell. The bell rang about half an hour later, and it was the ambassador. "André, I'm sorry. Here's five hundred dollars." I said, "Your Excellency, I don't want five hundred dollars. I just want to be treated with respect." After that I cooked for him for many years.

Every kitchen when I was a young chef had an omelet pan. We had kept it on a nail on the wall. You could use it for nothing else than omelet; if you cooked other things in them they would stick. It was always very clean. It never went to the dishwasher. We made our omelet and then we put a little coarse salt in and we wiped it out and put it back on the nail. We don't need it anymore. Now we have nonstick. If you keep the tines of the fork pointed away from the Teflon, you should be okay. But my approach to cooking, my philosophy, is all in the omelet. That shows me attention and craft. When I see a cook make an omelet, I see whether they can apply themselves. Every gesture counts. If you put too much butter in the pan you'll have an omelet with a wrinkled surface. The food we did at Lutèce was exemplified by that approach. It was classic, it was regional, and it had the lightness that only care brings.

Of course, because we were an elegant restaurant we had to have foie gras and truffles, and some people would have liked to have those ingredients on everything. I often would say, "These poor rich people, they can't eat the real food." For me the real food was more basic. Every day for lunch I did a plat du jour. That's when I did what I call the real cooking. And that's what people like most. It was not on the menu. I couldn't put a recipe like my mother's *tourte aux pommes the terre*, a potato tart on the menu. You layer potatoes and hardboiled eggs in a thin crust. The food cost was a few cents. My plats du jour were Alsatian oriented, like *matelote au Riesling*. But we also did cuisine bourgeois dishes like navarin and boeuf à la mode. I used to go out to

233

the dining room and tell people about these dishes. I'd say, "Today we have a nice little *coq sauté à la biere*," and people loved that.

You have to train yourself to be comfortable in the dining room. We chefs are a little shy. We're always scared that they'll say they didn't like it. It's not easy when you ask, "How did you like your meal?" and they say, "We didn't." Most of the time you can iron it out. Maybe they say something was oversalted or undersalted. When people are happy, it's nice to go out and see them, but it's when people are unhappy that you really have to do it. Or else in their minds it gets worse and worse.

I worked fourteen to sixteen hours a day, six days a week, all my life. When people came looking for a job, I never asked where they worked before. I looked at them. If we made contact, I said to them, "I'm looking for somebody. You can work for me. I will work for you, too." I wanted them to learn to do things our way, to work cleanly and with discipline. Starting at nine meant starting at ten minutes before nine not five minutes after. I also treated people well. I had people working for me for thirty years. I gave people insurance, and we had profit sharing for everyone, dishwashers and cooks. I started with health insurance because in France we have good insurance, and profit sharing because it's good for the ambience and people work better.

One of the proudest days of my life was when I got the Meilleur Ouvrier de France award. My mother was able to see it. It means you are the best craftsman in your discipline for that year. It meant more to me than when I received the Légion d'Honneur. Why? Because for me it is all about craft. I don't want to hear about artists. We chefs, we don't want to be artists; we want to be craftsmen. One day an artist does something beautiful; the next day he puts what he does in a drawer for a week. We have to produce every day, twice a day, and you have to be ready at noon and six thirty, and only a craftsman can do that.

I think it's important for cooks not to lose perspective. That was always true, but it is particularly so today. It's not because we cook for ambassadors that we are ambassadors. I used to tell my partner, André Surmain, "André, we are soup merchants. We make soup and we sell soup." For chefs today it is a big danger. They get on TV once or twice and some of them can't handle it. I got lots of offers to open other Lutèce restaurants. A Japanese company wanted me to open seven in Japan. I always said no. Simone and I were okay. We were modest people. We didn't need much. In Paris we didn't even live in an apartment; we lived in a room. My generation stayed in the kitchen. Did you ever go to the theater and the star wasn't there? You didn't enjoy it so much. My philosophy is if they came to your restaurant, you were there.

I still have my chef's knife from my apprenticeship. Its wood handle is long gone. But if I try I can see many things reflected in its blade. I can see a boy who cycled through country roads with a backpack of chef's vests for his mother to wash. I can see a chef who was welcomed into a country whose openness allowed him to succeed. I also see some of the mysteries of the profession, because cooking ultimately comes from the inside. It takes discipline and a little talent, but also love. You have to cook with pleasure because it's by cooking with pleasure that we chefs can show love. I had customers who when they left they kissed me. They paid me and then they kissed me. I wouldn't have wanted to miss that.

Jacques Torres

Jacques Torres is one of the world's most famous pastry chefs. He began his career in a small pastry shop in his native Bandol, moved to a position at La Cadière d'Azur, and later spent eight years with Jacques Maximin at the Hôtel Negresco in Nice. Upon moving to the United States, Torres was hired by the Ritz-Carlton Hotel, and later became the executive pastry chef at Le Cirque. He opened Jacques Torres Chocolate, a chocolate factory in Brooklyn, and Chocolate Haven, in Manhattan. He has published several books and hosted numerous television shows. The James Beard Foundation awarded Torres with Pastry Chef of the Year, and he is currently the dean of pastry arts at The French Culinary Institute.

You can fit all of Bandol into Central Park. It's a small town in Provence that people in the U.S. might have heard of because we make a good rosé. That's my town. I wanted to be a chef when I was fifteen. I wanted to cook. But there was no big restaurant in Bandol that I could work at while I did an apprenticeship. There was, however, a good pastry shop. One day I went in and asked the owner, "Can I try? Can I try on Wednesday on the way to school, and on Sunday?" He accepted that, though he didn't know much about me except I had the gumption to go in and ask.

This was just after Christmas and they were making *galette des rois,* the kings' cake, for the Feast of the Epiphany. In the south of France we make those big brioches and we put fruit confit on top and lots of glaze. So it's sticky because of the glaze, and you have it on your hands, and you open the fridge, and now the fridge has it, and then sheet pans have it. That first Sunday I fell in love with it. I just fell in love with that job. It's sticky, it's sweet, it's fun, and it makes people happy.

For the pastry professional, it is also addictive. When you come in at five in the morning, and you open the door and you smell the fermentation of the dough and the croissants coming out of the oven, right away you're hungry. And you're proud to be in a job that allows people a moment of joy. I fell in love with that world of pastry right away.

For my military service I asked to be a Chasseur Alpin. This is a legendary regiment of the army where basically they put a backpack and skis on your back and you have to go up the mountain for hours and come down in five minutes and start back up again. It was crazy, but I asked for it because I wanted to do some sports. When I came out of the military I decided to try and find work in Nice because my girlfriend was there. I was walking with her one day on the Promenade des Anglais, the gardens right beside the coast, and I saw the beautiful Hôtel Negresco. In French they call these great luxury hotels *les palaces,* because with all their balconies and their elegance they really do look like palaces. It's pretty scary to go into those places when you're a young boy from Bandol. But I made a bet with my girlfriend. I said, "I bet you that I can go ask for a job in there." It was like a joke.

I walked over to the big entrance. The *voiturier*, or doorman, had a big hat with a feather in it, and I said to him, "I'm looking for a job." He almost had a fit. "No, no, no. Not here. You have to go in the back of the hotel. This is not the entrance for that."

So I went to the back of the hotel and talked to the *chef de personnel*. He said, "Pastry, yes, we need someone in pastry. Come with me." So he escorted me to the kitchen. I'd never been in a restaurant kitchen before that. I worked in a pastry shop. I remember all the hanging copper pots, all the cooks in white with the toques, the silence. It was a classic kitchen in France. The thirty-two-year-old chef, Jacques Maximin, was in his office wearing a white shirt open all the way to his belly button and smoking a cigarette. He looked at me like "What do you want?" I said, "I just finished my military service and I'm looking for a job." That guy is always wired. He looked at me again and he said, "If you're good, I'll keep you. If you're not good—out." I kind of got offended at being spoken to like that. I said, "Fine, no problem." I think he liked that reaction. He liked to see me standing up like that. So he said, "Okay, come back in an hour with a jacket and pants. You're starting right away." So I went out and I said to my girlfriend, "What do I do? The guy just hired me." We ran around looking for a jacket and pants for me, and that day I started an eight-year journey at one of the greatest places in the south of France.

Chef and pastry chef are two different animals. I liken it to medicine: A chef is like the emergency room doctor. They have to react, they have to be fast, they're under fire and they have to deal with it. The pastry chef is different; they cannot do things at the last minute. They need to have things almost finished. So the pastry chef is more like the specialist who perhaps takes care of the knee. I think when you are a pastry chef

you have to recognize that you are always second to the chef. That's the way it is. Now keep in mind that what you do the chef cannot do, because that's your specialty. You're an expert on it. So the chef needs you. Ideally that makes for common respect. I think that's the best scenario: you work together with the chef and not for someone who knows less than you do driving you to do things they can't.

Maximin and I actually liked each other. He always respected me, and I regard him as a great chef. From the beginning he said, "You should do the MOF." The Meilleur Ouvrier de France is a competition that is held every three years which, if you win, gives you the honor to wear the tricolor on the collar of your chef's jacket and be called the best craftsman. He was one in cooking and he encouraged me to enter the pastry competition. "No way," I'd say. "It takes too much work, too much energy, too much talent." You can't enter the competition before you're twenty-six, and it so happened that the year of my twenty-sixth birthday and the year of the competition coincided. One day I said, "You know what, I'm going to give it a shot." And I did. A great friend, Louis "Lulu" Franchin, trained me. I'd stay in the kitchen in the afternoon to do sugar and chocolate work.

They tell you the subject you're going to be given one month before the competition, so for that whole month I worked, worked, worked, and lived like a monk. The morning of the competition everybody was telling me, "Jacques, you have to stay very clean." Well, when you're a pastry chef, you always make your sleeves dirty, and so those sleeves always bothered me because they drag. Before the competition, I took scissors and I cut the sleeves, and I asked my mom to quickly hem them. That's not quite the look you're supposed to have. During the competition the president of the jury came over, looked at me, and he said, "Are you on vacation here?" I looked at him and I said, "You know, I'm from the south of France. That's what we wear over there." So I was the kid of the competition, and perhaps I was less stressed than everyone, and Lulu had trained me pretty hard, but after three days of competition, when they gave the results, they called me as the winner. I was not ready for that, and my jacket was not clean when I went up to the podium. But I felt very proud.

I came to the U.S. to do some consulting with Jacques Maximin in Laguna Niguel, California. I liked the feel of California because it's a bit like Provence. So I decided it would be a challenge if I stayed in America for a while. I talked to a chef that I know from the Ritz-Carlton, and they hired me to open the Ritz-Carlton in Rancho Mirage. I went there and stayed six months, and then I spent another six months in another Ritz-Carlton, in Atlanta. One day Daniel Boulud called and asked me if I would go to New York. I was not really interested in working in New York; it was too big a city. But Alain Ducasse called me (we all know each other; what can I say?) and he said, "Jacques, what are you doing? Things happen in New York. Things that don't happen anywhere else. You have to go to New York." So I did. I spoke to Sirio Maccioni and I spent twelve years at Le Cirque with Daniel, and Sylvain Portay and Sottha Khunn.

I learned many things working at Le Cirque. But certainly among the most important ones was that you shouldn't just look at plates as they go out; you should look at them when they come back, too. At

241

Le Cirque the dishwashing station was directly across from the pastry station, so I always saw the dishes coming back. I knew exactly which were the favorites, from both the sweet and savory sides. That's the best way for anyone in a kitchen to know if customers like what you're doing. That's really listening to the customer. Because most times when you go out and talk to people, you're wearing your whites, and it's a nice moment and people don't want to ruin it by saying something negative. So, in cooking, you're really kind of listening when you look.

One of the highlights of my time there was making a dessert for a special party for Pierre Franey, who was like the elder statesman of all the French chefs. They were all going to be at it. What do you do for a chef? Those guys eat, know, and see everything, and I thought about it until finally I had it. Pierre Franey spent his life in front of a stove. Why not build a stove? So I built a big stove in sugar, real size, with the pots and everything, all in sugar. Then I did smaller individual ones for dessert. I put a burner and pots and an oven door, and every part of it was edible. Everyone loved it—I watched the plates come back to make sure—and we decided to put it on the menu. A dessert like that is a big challenge, because it's pretty complicated, but it became Le Cirque's signature dessert, along with the crème brûlée, of course.

Gradually I started to come back to chocolates. I felt something fascinating was going on in chocolate in America. When I first came here, chocolate was like coffee. A cup of coffee was a cup of coffee and a piece of chocolate was a piece of chocolate. Now, I love M&Ms. I love their colors. When you open a package, it's just a happy feeling. But I wanted to approach it at the artisanal level, where you are constantly dealing with all the variables that go into the making of top-level chocolate.

You start from cacao beans. They can come from many places in the world. Venezuela. Trinidad is good, and some of the islands around Trinidad, too. Madagascar, on the coast of Africa, is also a very good origin. Ivory Coast and Ghana produce about forty percent of the world's cacao today, but it's not as highly regarded as that from South or Central America. The kind of tree is going to play a role, too. There are three different kinds of trees: criollo, trinitario, and forastero. The criollo is very rare; the tree produces less than ten percent of the world's chocolates, and its beans cost about three times the price of regular beans. It will give you something with a lot of flair and some citrus flavor. It's a little whimsical, a little crazy; the chocolate seems to be going in every direction. When you have African beans, the chocolate is a lot calmer. It's a lot earthier, and you know what to expect.

By the time I get the beans, they've already been fermented. The first thing that I'm going to do is roast them. So I roast in small batches and I taste it. And when the chocolate becomes nutty, that's when the chocolate is ready, so every batch can be a little bit different. I cool it down, and then I put it to a machine to remove the shell, and I get what we call the nibs. Those nibs are going to be ground into a paste, and we call that cacao paste or cacao liquor. The better the cacao liquor, the less sugar that we add to the chocolates. So it really depends on where the chocolates come from, where the beans come from, how they have been fermented, and how they have been roasted. If everything goes well, I will do a seventy to seventy-five percent cacao content in chocolates, where we really get the flavor of that chocolate. Less expensive chocolates have a lot more sugar because the quality of the beans isn't there and you have to put something else in.

I won't tell you that I knew all this when I was a pastry chef. I had to teach myself a lot of it. I didn't go to a school because there's not really a school to learn that, so I learned by making, and I tried to see what level, what stage, is the most difficult. Well, there isn't one. If you don't roast well, chocolate is bad. If you forget some shells, chocolate is bad. If you make a mistake with the recipe, chocolate is bad. Every stage is critical, so I made a lot of bad chocolates. I gave a lot of bad chocolate to friends. They aren't personal friends anymore. It took me a lot of tries to make a good chocolate, and finally, slowly, I started to make chocolate that I was happy with.

I guess I've always loved a challenge because then I decided to leave the restaurants and open my own chocolate factory. I found a location in Brooklyn, which wasn't the hip borough it is today. We opened just before Christmas 2000. The paint literally wasn't dry. We had a few chocolates displayed on the counter, and one gentleman came in. He looked at the chocolates, he asked for a box of them, he took out twenty dollars, and he took his chocolate and left. When he was out of sight, a few of us performed a little happy dance behind the counter.

Today we go through a hundred tons of chocolate a year. We have expanded to a second location, in Manhattan on Hudson Street, and I've been able to get old chocolate manufacturing equipment, which for me has a lot of soul. My favorite is a forty-year-old wrapping machine from Switzerland. It's enormous, two and a half tons. Sometimes it wraps very well with no problems. And sometimes, it's impossible to make it run. So it's very funny now. When we start work with it we pat it, we talk nicely to it, then we start to put bars in and we all look at it. Sometimes the bars come out nicely wrapped. But sometimes the machine doesn't want to run. We stop and then the next day we try again. We used to call that machine the old lady, and it didn't work very well, so we changed that to the Queen Mary. Now that we've given her a nicer name she tends to work a lot better.

The store is in the middle of the factory. It is surrounded by glass, and customers can come in and watch us do all the processes. For me, it was important that people see us and understand that chocolate is something with a culture and with its own seasons. Easter, for example, is one of those holidays where, in addition to eggs, we do a lot of figures like rabbits and chickens. We fill the store with all those things. I have tall rabbits, roosters with beautiful colors, chickens for the baskets, and all those beautiful eggs. When you go to the store at Easter you find chocolates everywhere, even hanging from the ceiling. So it's really a sense of happiness during Easter. And that goes for five or six weeks and then when Easter is done we wash all the molds and put everything back until the next year. So we do it once a year. That's it. For the past five years my friend and teacher Lulu comes from Nice and helps us. He stays with us for five weeks, and we have a good time and I really cherish that time with him.

People love to come in because the place makes them happy just as chocolate is supposed to do. But I think there is also a question of scale that people respond to more and more. People like to see the person behind a product. I'm fascinated by how Hershey and Mars can do millions of bars, but that is not what I set out to do. I'm an artisan. In Bandol, I knew the fisherman and I knew the vegetable seller and the shoe seller. Each product had a face which I could put on it. I wanted people to put a face on chocolate. For me, that is really what *artisanal* means. There are times when we're all standing around the Queen Mary holding our breath until we see how the first bars will come out, and I have to say to myself, "If this isn't artisanal, I don't know what is."

245

Charlie Trotter

Charlie Trotter is the chef and owner of the highly acclaimed Chicago restaurant Charlie Trotter's, hailed by *Wine Spectator Magazine* as the "Best Restaurant in the World for Wine & Food," and "America's Best Restaurant." It has received five stars from Mobil, five diamonds from AAA, and seven awards from the James Beard Foundation. Trotter opened Trotter's to Go and C, a fine-dining seafood restaurant in Mexico. Author of ten cookbooks, Trotter is also the host of the award-winning PBS show *The Kitchen Sessions with Charlie Trotter.* He is involved in a number of charities, including the Charlie Trotter Culinary Education Foundation.

All through his high school and college years my father was a jazz trumpeter. He was either going to name me after Miles Davis or after Charlie Parker. I guess by the time my mother was pregnant, he'd decided. He'd pat her on the tummy and say, "How's Charlie doing?" and she didn't know why. To this day I don't think she realizes that one of the reasons he married her is because her name is Donna Lee, and that was one of the great Charlie Parker songs. And so I'm named after Charlie Parker, and I take much of my inspiration from jazz greats like John Coltrane and Charlie Parker and Miles Davis. The Midwest played its own kind of role in my naming also. When I was ten years old I went to sports camp, and the counselor said, "What's your name?" "I'm Charlie Trotter," I answered. "You're not a Charlie," he said. "You're a Chuck." So for the next six or so years I was known as Chuck Trotter. To this day, when someone calls up the restaurant and says, "I'm an old friend of Chuck's," we know they really have known me a long time and we get them in.

My mom was a good cook, but I wouldn't call her a gourmet cook. She was probably ahead of her time in that in the sixties and in Chicago she would serve fish a couple nights a week. She had a repertoire of maybe ten dishes that just kept recycling themselves, but food was never a big deal. It was Middle America in the 1960s. We'd go out for my mom's birthday and my parents' anniversary or high school graduation, but it was nothing fancy. I think my level of interest was, oh, this is great. You can get your own lobster tail with drawn butter.

My dad founded a company that was an upper-level executive recruitment firm with offices all over North America. Not that I even really understood what he did. At an early age in my life he said, "You can do whatever you want, just remember, you're never going to come to work for me, because you'll never be happy if you go into work for the old man. Ultimately, you're only going to be happy if you are your own boss, that is, you're controlling your own destiny." So, from an early age, I began to think, well, I'm going to have to pick my own thing. Only years later did I realize how blessed I was to have parents who trusted me to find my own way.

I went to the University of Wisconsin at Madison and studied philosophy and political science. I had a roommate who used to cook all the time. He'd make bread and pasta from scratch and stuff sausage casings and check on his homemade wine. I'd never seen things like this. So I began to cook with him, from books like Craig Claiborne's *New York Times Cookbook* and the Julia Child books and James Beard's *American Cookery*. Back then I thought that cooking was not unlike a math problem, in that you had to measure everything meticulously and not deviate. If it said, "braise the duxelle of mushroom five minutes," I practically timed it on a stopwatch.

But pretty soon I realized that you really could adjust things. In fact, I realized that that adjustment of ingredients with a specific goal in mind was something I loved to do. So I thought, well, what if I go into cooking? What's the worst that can happen? I mean, food and the pleasures of the table is something that we all enjoy every day, and great things happen around the table with family and friends. I was actually more interested in the sensual pleasures than necessarily the intellectual pleasures of the table at that time. And so I thought, if I do this for three or four years, cook in restaurants and work in dining rooms, I'll find out whether I'm any good at it or even if I like it. If I don't, I can always go back to college, go to graduate school, or maybe business school, or I can find something else that I'd like to do. But it won't have been wasted time. I will have informed myself on how to cook, and this will apply for the rest of my life. So I had no grandiose ambition.

I'm not sure my parents were—how should I say this?—down with it. But they said, "You know, if you're happy, we're happy for you, and you have to find what you want to do in life." And so I started out in the profession. I was a busboy, a waiter, a barman, and eventually a cook. The first job I ever had in a kitchen was under Norman Van

Aken. We're like brothers in a way, because we love literature and music as much as we love gastronomy, and we're both avid readers. I was twenty-two years old, and I thought, you know, I can't believe they're willing to pay me $3.10 an hour. These people are crazy. I should be paying them to be here.

Eventually I would work in many restaurants. I always had this idea that I'd stay as long as I continued to learn. It might be three years; it might be much less. Whatever length of time it was, my attitude was always, whenever I leave a place, they're going to have to hire two people to replace me, because I believe you don't just take, you have to give. And so I approached every job the same way. Whatever the start time is, if it's four in the afternoon, I'm going to be there at noon. If it's two in the afternoon, I'm going to be there at nine in the morning, because it's about learning, and you never, ever stop learning. Sometimes I'll see people that get caught up in "Well, what's the title or what's the salary?" And I'll say, "Don't even worry about that. You've got so many years to focus on the learning side of it. Take advantage of that. It will pay off in huge ways that you can't even imagine at this time."

If I had to name the top four or five experiences of my career, number one would be the fact that for the first seven years of my restaurant's operation I got to work with my father every single day. I observed in him characteristics of excellence that I was able to take and apply to the restaurant world. At first, he didn't understand cooks. He'd say, "Who are the people who are drawn to this field? They're disorganized; they stay out late." But he was a detail fanatic. He'd roll in every morning at seven. I'd have gotten out at two thirty, and by the time I came in he'd be waiting for me. "Did you get back to this person? Did you notice that person would have preferred something else? Have you called them yet?"

In that way he was instrumental in laying the foundation of the restaurant. Charlie Trotter's is a restaurant that is concerned not with the bottom line but with the top line. I have a nasty spending habit, and I will always be looking for china and stemware. Sometimes you just want to be a little deeper in '45 Mouton. But it goes so much further than that. I want the restaurant to represent an ideal of excellence. That doesn't mean blind perfection, which I find kind of sterile. I mean true excellence, a sincerity of effort and a wish for everyone who works there to come in every day and try and improve a little bit from the day before.

It starts with how we hire. We come straight out and ask, "Why are you interviewing for this position?" If people say, "Well, I want to be a manager." I ask them, "Why would you want to be a manager when you can be a leader?" It's a lot more profound to be on the road to leadership than on the road to management. Your standards for yourself have to be higher than anything the restaurant can ask of you. And so we instill in people this idea, this ethic, that leadership is your ultimate challenge. At that time you must regard yourself as working for yourself. You're not working for a supervisor or the maître d' or the chef de cuisine—you are, in a sense, because we may ask you to do this or that, but, really, you are working for yourself, and as high as my standards may be for you, your own standards for yourself have to be even higher.

That approach has a dramatic influence on the restaurant's atmosphere. We don't use those classic expressions of "front-of-house team," "back-of-house team." Each member of our kitchen team

spends a week at a time in the dining room, and conversely our dining room team spends a week in the kitchen, because we're all just one
team. I've worked in restaurants where the poor service staff member
would come into the kitchen with a plate of fish or a rack of lamb
and literally trembling go up to the chef. "I'm sorry but the lady says
it's too undercooked." They're ready for the reply that goes, "That's
not my problem. They should have ordered something else!" What
oftentimes chefs don't understand is that the job on the service side
is harder than the job in the kitchen. Out there they have to maintain
an emotional high and be attuned to every need and nuance of a client, and they actually have to be there on the battle line and deal with
what goes on. In our kitchen waiters don't even have to give an expla-
nation. So our service team member is very comfortable coming in
and saying, "I made a mistake. I forgot to mention that this person has

a shellfish allergy, could you remake the turbot without the clams?" "No problem. We'll get that for you right away." That way that person feels empowered in the dining room to do things spontaneously.

We live in a time when the personal touch is being once, twice, and five times removed from experiences and interactions we have. I don't ever want that to happen in the dining room. We like to say that our service team comes equipped with almost a bag of tricks. They come out and it's like an old-fashioned country doctor opening this bag up and pulling out the stethoscope and the tongue depressor and everything else. Our service team members know that they are empowered to do things for any guest at any time. That means if you come in during white truffle season you can really put a hit on us. And it's not exactly fun when someone decides it's imperative to open an eighteen-hundred-dollar bottle of wine for a table because they just think that's what it's going to take to push it over the edge—but they can. There's always something that can elevate a meal. Whether it's an extra dessert course, or champagne, or a tour of the kitchen or the wine cellar, or an esoteric wine poured in a nice glass, all these things can customize the dinner experience.

Excellence in the kitchen again starts with an approach. I've always said that you could determine whether you wanted to hire someone to be in your restaurant and never ask them to cook one thing. You could ask them to take a broom and sweep, and follow that up with mopping and spending five minutes at the dish machine. You can see an awareness and a sensitivity in those acts alone. There simply isn't a hierarchy of actions in my kitchen, where some can be performed carelessly and others with great attention. Not slamming the oven door is part of how I cook, and putting the Robot Coupe away properly so it's ready for the next person who uses it is part of how I cook, too. They really are just as important as sautéing a beautiful piece of fish. Carelessly performed acts will eventually lower the level of attention with which every gesture is performed. Then it becomes acceptable; then it becomes an atmosphere. The moment that happens, you've lost your focus. It's gone.

I take much of my inspiration from the jazz greats. I use Miles Davis or Charlie Parker as examples of artists or creative people whose art was constantly in flux. So Miles might play "Stella by Starlight," and then a week later, in a different club, he might play "Stella by Starlight" again, but he might have the band pick up the tempo. A week later he might not even emphasize his own horn, but the alto sax playing next to him. And a year later he might put a mute on his horn. And five years later he might play "Stella by Starlight" and he's now turned it into a loving ballad that's not five minutes but twelve minutes long. That, really, in a nutshell, summarizes how we approach food.

I might be working with rabbit and fava beans and morel mushrooms and mustard and tarragon this week, and even day to day I'll change it a little bit. We might emphasize a little more sweet or sour flavor as we're braising the morels, or we might adapt to the wines. If a wine that is being consumed is a crisp, light, young white wine, then the dish might be a little bit more vibrant. If the wine is a pinot noir, we might allow more concentrated meat juice, and so now we're pushing it into red wine territory. This is not change for the sake of change. It's change that comes naturally as a result of being in the moment and responding to ingredients. I've never been a fan of the "this is my dish" approach. This is the langoustine ravioli with this one sauce and I got written up for it and it's a crowd pleaser so I can't dream of changing it. I'm more of the school "I can't imagine that you wouldn't want to change it."

People who are drawn to this field are generous by nature. You're doing something for someone that's very personal and very elemental. You don't just say, "I'll throw it together, and here it is." So giving comes naturally to us. That said, a restaurant can easily feel overwhelmed by requests. Can you donate dinner for four? Can you donate dinner for six? When you have a small hundred-seat restaurant, or smaller, it is substantial to give away six percent of your gross for a night. We have devised a different kind of approach for that kind of thing. Most people that go to a charitable event could probably afford to write a check to the organization and come to buy dinner, so what we donate to live auctions is something called the Guest for a Day program, where people buy a behind-the-scenes look and we feed them and give them wine along the way and it is really memorable for them.

But we also want the restaurant to be part of the broader community. For that, we have a two-pronged approach. We started a foundation called the Culinary Education Foundation, which raises funds and gives scholarships for people entering the hospitality field. And we have also started something called the Excellence Program, which reaches out to the even broader community. Three times a week, for the past seven years, we've had twenty Chicago high school students come with two or three teacher chaperones. They ride on a school bus and are greeted at the front door, given a tour of the dining rooms, the wine cellars, and the kitchen. Then they sit in our studio kitchen at one big table, which is where we film our PBS series, and they have basically the same menu that's being served in the dining room that night. And if we're serving sweetbreads or if we're serving lamb tongue or we're serving cod cheeks, these young folks are having these items, too. Along the way, they hear from a dozen staff members, pastry chef, fish cook, sous-chef, sommelier, dining room leader, food runner, myself. Each individual from my staff describes how they pursue excellence every single day, how they try to go to the next level every single day. Then they field questions, and we go around the table until everyone asks two questions. We talk about all kinds of things, from sustainable farming to organic food products versus nonorganic, to how to work with humility, to the whole notion of you get what you give, and if you want a lot from life, you've got to give a lot.

For the first five years we were open, cooks would say to me, "Chef, what do I do here?" And I'd go, "Are they talking to me? Oh, I guess they are." I didn't like to go out to the dining room because I felt I would be intruding. Now I'm much more comfortable going out, and I understand that being greeted by the chef can make a person's evening. And I enjoy it, too. But you still have to be careful. You don't want to just approach and go, "Okay, well, here I am." If someone makes eye contact, then that's like a signal to go over. "Hi, how was everything? A little tour of the kitchen? Sure."

But it isn't just the bliss of after dinner that I enjoy. I like all times of the day in a restaurant kitchen. I like the days when we're not even open and I'm the only one in the whole building and I'm walking through and everything is pristine and in its place and you can almost feel the spirit of what's there and what's been there. And I like the kitchen in the early morning when there are only two or three people there, and the guy has several pots on the stove and is reducing things and braising vegetables and cutting up meat, and it's so quiet you can hear these beautiful noises. And someone in the pastry department is rolling out bread. And then I like it when it begins to build, and more chefs come, and I like the beginning of service, when there's this high anticipation, when it's almost like the tip-off of a basketball game. That is often a moment of clarity for me. I can feel the presence of people who have helped the restaurant become what it is. Like Reginald Watkinson, who was the first person I hired and is one of the key sous-chefs today. I can see the cooking profession itself, a craft that has allowed me to go inside myself and given me a means of expressing what I find. And just before the orders start coming in, I can see the restaurant in its broadest dimension. We have been open twenty years. If the day ever comes that we close, if we can say that we made an aesthetic, a cultural, and a social contribution to our city and our community, then we will have been excellent. We will have achieved our goal.

Norman Van Aken

Norman Van Aken is a forerunner of the culinary fusion movement, credited with creating the New World Cuisine, an approach to American cuisine that incorporates the United States' dynamic ethnic mix. Born in a small town in Illinois, Van Aken transformed several Florida restaurants into culinary destinations and eventually opened Norman's, in Coral Gables, and then others. He was awarded Best Chef in the Southeast by the James Beard Foundation and received the *Food Arts* Silver Spoon Lifetime Achievement Award. He is the author of four cookbooks, most recently *New World Kitchen*.

There was a period in the '70s when I was going back and forth between Key West and Illinois. I hitchhiked to Key West, loved it, ran out of money, came back to Illinois, and got a job in a diner. Janet was in high school waiting tables. I was the daytime guy, and she was working nights. One day I saw her, and it wasn't long before we were going out together. She grew up in a family of eight children, in a small house with one bathroom, a Polish Catholic girl. She grew up learning to cook watching her mother. She was fascinated by cooking. Her father, he was a great barbecue guy

259

and loved it. He'd stand out there in the snow, park his can of Schlitz on top of the Weber, put a little snow around it. He'd be out there with a cigarette between his lips flipping the ribs. Illinois cuisine.

Well, I guess Janet saw something in me, because it wasn't long before we went to Key West together. I got a job at a place called the Midget Bar and Grill, open twenty-four hours; I worked the grave-yard shift. There was a tree growing through the middle of the roof in that place. I had no idea how to cook the food, but an old chef called Sammy brutalized me until he taught me how to cook barbecue. One night I took Janet to Louie's Backyard for her birthday. It was origi-nally a home built for a ship's captain in 1909. This was years before I worked there. Afterward, I went to the Midget to go to work. Janet walked me over there. My dishwasher no-showed, and she washed dishes all night, on her nineteenth birthday, and we've been through the whole thing together. Our son, Justin, has been in many ways, too. Janet writes the books with me. If you can find someone who can share some aspect of this cooking life, it's a blessing for sure. It would be very hard to get through what is required of you to be a chef today without someone to share all those times with.

I think to be successful at cooking you have to have incredible hunger, no doubt about it, not just for food. No one thought about being a chef when I was growing up. That was not really there, but there was a hunger to find expression as an artist. I was drawn early on to biographies and to reading about people, and I think that life stories were something that made me feel that seemingly small things matter. I'd think, "Oh, look what that conversation meant or how that event changed them." So there's a hunger to want to become some-thing, to contribute, to do something that's good in the world. My feeling was that there is always too much friction in the world, too much fighting, too much nonsense, and too much tragedy.

I came from a home that was what they called a broken home—such a strong word. My father was a used-car dealer and my mother waited tables when they met. They had a stormy relationship. The first ten years of my life were great. Everything was sunny. I had wonderful sisters, a beautiful mother, and a handsome, dramatic father. We grew up in a fabulously bucolic place near the Wisconsin border, right on a lake. I tramped through the fields in the summer and slid down the hills in the winter. Then my mother and father broke up, and it's kind of hard on a kid. You just want to put them back together. That was a big thing in my life.

I ended up sort of drafted into the restaurant business a bit young. I was a busboy, dishwasher, helping my mom. That did not seem like the place where I could find the artistry that I was looking for. In some of the first places I worked one of my jobs would be, when the chef wasn't looking, to go to the liquor store and get the beer and *vino* and hide it in the coolers. Being the youngest person in the kitchen, the other cooks would tell me what to do. I could see that these men lived a life that was far from the glitter. It didn't take a genius to figure out that this was not necessarily a glorified life, where I would find a way of conveying any sense of artistry. As a matter of fact, there were times when it was just quite simply scary to see how these people would be destroying themselves.

I went to college for about two years. I sold flowers in Honolulu. I worked as a carnie, and got electrocuted by a Ferris wheel. It was working as a roofer that got me back into cooking. I got fired for laughing when a thunderstorm ended our work one afternoon. It was

261

a hundred degrees that day, and the storm broke through, and I was rolling around in the grass laughing, and the foreman said, "We don't need your kind around here." I was renting a house with some other guys and I needed to pay the rent. So I went to the newspaper. I saw a job for a short-order cook. I tied my hair and hid it underneath my collar and went to apply for the job. I got it, and I soon found out that they liked me, even though I had long hair. They liked the fact that I was trying. That waitress, I was going to get her food in the window. That cook, I was going to help him slice the ham and cheese and put it on paper. It kind of reminded me of what great, unbiased places kitchens can be.

When my mother and father were still together, for about three winters we went to Miami Beach on vacation. I have a strong memory of getting off a plane at age seven and staying at the art deco hotels on the beach, smelling people with suntan lotion and eating the first exotic fruits I'd ever tasted and feeling that sense of pleasure and escape that the world in various places can offer. It hit a strong note with me. It was when I was old enough to go on my own that I hitch-hiked to Key West. It was post-Vietnam and right around Watergate, and I really wanted to get away from all the things I felt were dark and discomforting about our country. I wanted to go someplace where there were real people and artists sort of cohabitating, and that was Key West. I could relate to all the fishermen and the writers and paint-ers and sculptors and characters. I was a cook and I had a little bit of an ability at it. But I had never been to culinary school. Even though I had always read, it had never crossed my mind to read a book or magazine on the subject. I cooked because it was something I got paid to do.

In 1978 I went to a job interview at the Pier House in Key West. I'd been cooking since 1972 and I really needed this job. I was bad broke. But I'd been hearing about the Pier House and how graduates of The Culinary Institute of America were doing things like mirepoix. I didn't know it was onions and carrots and celery cooked down and used as a base for sauces. I had no idea what mirepoix was. So I got there for the interview, and it was just before service. There was a chocolate cake sitting on a table, and the chef came out of her office swearing like crazy. "All right, I'll taste the damned cake. Put it up there." The pastry chef puts up the cake. She cuts it, puts a piece in her mouth, she gets this look on her face like she's happy, then she takes the knife and knocks the cake into the garbage can. "We're not serving that here." And I thought, "Holy cow, these people are intense. They care about what they're doing. I want this job."

So I got a job cooking breakfast. Shortly thereafter I moved up and I became the line guy at night. There was a guy over me and one day he was leaning against the big Hobart mixer and he used a culinary term, and I had no idea what it meant. That really pissed me off because he didn't strike me as any kind of genius, and I said, "Hooker, how do you even know that word?" It was velouté. And he said, "Because I went to The Culinary Institute of America, in Hyde Park." "Yeah, I'm aware," I said. "How much does that cost? Tell me again." I think he said thirty-five thousand dollars or some astronomical figure. I said, "Well, that's about as real as a moon shot for me. What else can I do?" And he goes, "Well, why don't you read books?" And I was like, "I read books. I read Dostoevsky, Hooker. What have you read?" He said, "Cookbooks. Why don't you read cookbooks?" And I said, "Who?" and he says, "Why don't you read James Beard."

263

That afternoon I stopped off at a bookstore on Duval Street and picked up *Theory and Practice of Good Cooking*. The book was not laid out in terms of soups, salads, appetizers, entrées, but broiling, grilling, sautéing, braising, and roasting. For the first time, I felt like I had someone whispering in my ear and telling me why we do things a certain way. It was 1979, and I began to educate myself. I had two knives, and every time I had some extra money I bought a book. I bought a book until I had a little desk and it had twelve cookbooks on it. For me, they were more than books, I felt in many ways that I went to jail for the wrong crime, and the only way I could get out of jail was by becoming a lawyer in jail, reading books. I knew I was never going to be able to go to cooking school, and I knew the only way I was going to make any money in this profession was to learn more, and so I became the cookbook junkie I still am today.

There were a number of books that came out around that time showcasing the nouvelle cuisine movement. There was one called *The Great Chefs of France,* where they went to twelve three-star restaurants. It was a huge picture book and I studied every picture and I'd look in the corners to see what they were doing. I can still see Jean Troisgros reaching over a table and a commis reaching under his arm; they were in the midst of the battle, and this was very exciting for me. So I'd be in my little kitchen with a chef's knife holding open a book and I'd be trying to make recipes from books like these. It's scary when you have no one to tell you whether you're making it right or wrong. At the same time, this period was just huge for me in terms of getting all the influences going and learning not only tasting but also seeing. I could see my cooking was becoming clearer, and I could see my sauces—it took me quite a while to say "my sauces"—but I could

see if they were right just by looking at them. It's a great period when you're assessing and studying and you learn to shut out lots of things. You no longer say, "This took me so long to make. It was hard to do." Bullshit. You now say, "This tastes right or it doesn't taste right." You now know that's the only thing that matters. You have to become a very severe critic of your work when you're learning by yourself.

Janet ended up getting homesick for Illinois, and we went back up when our son, Justin, was one. I got a job in a restaurant in Lake Forest, working for Gordon Sinclair. He had one of the first restaurants to declare itself to be a New American Cuisine restaurant, not that we really knew what that meant. The bicentennial may have had something to do with it, but there was something in the air. Paul Prud-homme was in New Orleans and Jasper White and Lydia Shire were in Boston. Gordon would go to the Coach House or the Four Seasons in New York, or he'd go to Spago or Chez Panisse, and he'd come back and just leave their books or menus on the counter for me. We came up with this promotion that we called a whistle-stop tour of America, where every week we basically pretended to go to a different location and create a true evocation of that location, whether it was Maine, Alaska, or Hawaii. Essentially it started with pure enthusiasm. It was just pretty much "Wow, let's get into this. Let's go. Let's discover American cuisine."

And then, magically, one day Gordon said, "Would you like to return to Florida? Because we're going to do a hotel project down there." Janet had gotten terribly done with being homesick, and we said, yes. So we returned to Florida and to a hotel. I hated it. There was one restaurant, so I wanted to do this New American cuisine and yet still had to cook hot dogs and hamburgers, because there was a pool and kids. One year later I got a job offer to go back to Key West, and this is really where the rubber met the road.

The chef at Louie's Backyard worked in his bare feet—he did a few things that you shouldn't do. In 1985 they hired me to take his place, and I did. The going away and the coming back had helped shift my thinking around in a more heightened way, and for the first time I really began to pose the question to myself: Why? Why do I cook what I do? Louie's sits right on the water. The deck looks out over the Gulf of Mexico. I was down there one morning reading Paula Wolfert and Roger Vergé and some other books, and I'm looking through them trying to think of specials. I look out at the water, and there's a boat going over the horizon. And I started to really think about the people on that boat and where they were going and where they had come from,, and I began to wonder what they would eat when they got there. And I realized they were probably going to Cuba. And I thought, why am I cooking Cajun food, and why am I cooking cioppino and dishes like that? Basically I said, "What am I doing? I should be thinking about where I live and letting those voices and those flavors come through me and find expression."

I immediately decided to go back to the little restaurants of Key West that I'd eaten at years earlier and sort of decode this rustic, Caribbean, Bohemian, African food and fuse it with what I had learned studying the French. I went to these little cafés and I sat there with my notepad and I would ask the people who were sitting with me at the counter what they were eating. The cop, the waitress, the gentleman with his kid having a sandwich. So I started to weave things like *ropa vieja* or fried plantains or other tropical fruits into Louie's menu. We might have had a veal chop but rubbed with adobo. I might have made a reduction sauce for a meat dish but made a kind of South American salsa that would have gone over it, to sort of whack it both ways. The term *fusion cooking* for me was not taking French and Thai and putting them together. For me, *fusion* was to take haute cuisine and peasant cuisine and fuse them.

If you think that's hard in France, try doing it in the Caribbean. You're talking about the sweep of history that is four or five hundred years long. And much of it is dark. The Spanish and the Portuguese "discoverers" essentially ran full riot over the indigenous people. The search for gold, the search for souls, the dominion that they held over the indigenous people, was incredible. And then fast after that, for a long period of time—forget the English, forget the Dutch, forget the French; they had very little to do with indigenous cuisine. It was slaves. There are estimates that ten million Africans were brought in

267

chains to do fieldwork, so the African influence on this cuisine was as vital and involved as the Spanish influence on this cuisine.

If Louie's was where I got the awareness behind New World cuisine, the next restaurant I worked at, Mira, is where it would be born. It was only about fifty seats and there were about three of us on that line and it was life or death. It's when the menu is you. It's not like there's Norman and there's the menu. They're symbiotic. You wake up to create the menu and you go to sleep with the menu in your mind. You dream of remaking the menu and then you start the next day and do it again. And you're really creating yourself. You're putting yourself out to the world, and the menu is the physical piece of paper. The most simple adjustments are huge. It's like "No, no, this is not the personality I want you to understand about me." I didn't think about money. I didn't think about food cost. I thought, what am I trying to say here? I really understood the artistic part of cooking, because some of those dishes simply had to find expression outside my head. I had to get them out right and I had to be honest about them and passionate.

It was a small kitchen. I entered through the side door on Simonton Street. The sautée station, which is where I worked, was right beside a window, and the sun would pour through that window like a blazing light right across the station. There was a girl named Kelly, who made salads, and another woman named Susan, who is the chef there now, who worked the grill and assisted me on plates. I worked the sauté and ran the tickets, and all the food went down the end of the line to a hole, where it was picked up. There was no air-conditioning. There is never air-conditioning in any of these places. I wore a thermometer around my neck and drank chocolate milk incessantly. It wasn't pretty, but the kitchen of Mira was one of those places you come to sometimes in life where you're either going to die or something's going to live. One of the two.

It's funny, sometimes you feel like you compete with your past. You want to struggle, to become new all over again, do new things, and then your customers, your guests, are almost like fans at an Eagles concert, saying, "Sing 'Desperado'!" There are dishes that if I'd known when I created that dish that I'd be cooking it fifteen or twenty years later, I may have stopped myself. But I think what has been achieved has been significant. I feel that what I did was give plates not so much a voice but a story; I cobbled together stories out of the things that I loved to taste from a region that had not been given that expression before.

Janet and I have bought a home back in Key West, and we're opening two restaurants in a resort. We've done the big-business thing in other places, and now I feel we've returned. There are only two places in my life where I feel I can walk these streets and I can be healed by them. They're the little lanes of Key West that are right along the shoreline. The fragrance of the flowers in the yards and the ocean is very captivating. When you're away from that and you come back to it, it knocks you over. I can look in the sky and see these amazing clouds and I just feel this is my place. I also feel it in the place where I was born and lived until I was sixteen, up in Illinois. I can walk through that area and still feel right. The rest of the world, I'm visiting, passing through, collecting data, information, notes, experiencing different things. But where I have the best sense of who I am is in those two places. I'm still that person who kept buying books. I am still curious. I am still hungry. I still keep dreaming that things can be put back together. And sometimes in restaurants they can.

Jean-Georges Vongerichten

Born and raised in Strasbourg, Jean-Georges Vongerichten started his career at the French restaurant Auberge de l'Ill, under Paul Haeberlin. He burst onto the New York scene at Lafayette, earning four stars from the *New York Times* at the age of twenty-nine. Vongerichten eventually opened several restaurants in New York, including Jean-Georges, Nougatine, JoJo, Mercer Kitchen, Vong, 66, Spice Market, and Perry Street. He opened Vong's Thai Kitchen in Chicago, Bank in Houston, Prime Steakhouse in Las Vegas, and restaurants in the Bahamas, London, Paris, and Shanghai. He has received Best New Restaurant and Outstanding Chef awards from the James Beard Foundation.

The coal barges used to come along a canal to the back of our house in Alsace. We were coal handlers, distributing coal for the city of Strasbourg. Gradually, as things changed, we went from coal to wood to gasoline to central heating installation. At lunch my mother and grandmother would cook for up to twenty-five people, family and employees. I loved the scene. Even as young as eight, I was always organizing little parties for my brothers and sister and cousins. But I was the oldest of three boys and one girl, and when I was twelve my father said, "I took over the business from my father and I want you to take it over from me." I was frustrated. I hated it. The business was in our house, and our lives were surrounded by coal.

I started in engineering school when I was fourteen. I couldn't apply myself, and eventually they threw me out. It was a bad situation. I was not good enough for school; the successor was not the successor. My father didn't talk to me for a year. Still, for my sixteenth birthday my parents took me to the Auberge de l'Ill, a Michelin three-star restaurant in Alsace. I suppose my mother pushed my father to take me. It was an eye-opener; I couldn't believe people were making a living from food. I came home and knew this was what I wanted to do, but I didn't tell my father because at the time he was ready to kill me. I was working for him and one day I went to him and I said, "I'm done. I'm not going to take over your business." He was furious. I said, "I want to cook in that restaurant you took me to six months ago." So I wrote a letter to the Haeberlin brothers—a very passionate letter, because I wanted to leave home. It is the only letter I've written looking for a job, and they took me in as an apprentice. That was 1973.

At the Auberge de l'Ill the food was Alsatian food done in the grandest style. It was fantastic. I really learned about the importance of ingredients there. To get milk we used to go to the farmers. If a trout order came in you had to go get it in the lake in the back. Whole deer would be brought into the kitchen. We had to skin rabbits. We had stocks and soups that would be simmering for hours. I learned a lot during my three-year apprenticeship and then I stayed an extra year so I could really master all the stations; and then I felt I was ready to move on. When you enter the Michelin three-star world it's like entering the mafia: with one phone call you have another job. So one call from Monsieur Haeberlin to Louis Outhier at L'Oasis, in La Napoule, and I was headed to the south of France.

Louis Outhier's cooking was all about the sun. I mean his cooking responded to the freshness of the sun, and I was really looking forward to learning about rosemary and thyme and olive oil. But my first lesson was that I had to forget everything I had learned. I mean *everything*: if I peeled an apple going around the apple, they wanted it peeled going up and down. I think it's really important for a young cook to be able to do that. It is not really forgetting what they've learned before but understanding that every technique used in a kitchen is part of the vision of the chef. You're not really forgetting; you're putting aside. It all adds to the depth of your knowledge.

Louis Outhier was a clean freak. He wanted nothing on the stove. So at twelve o'clock we had nothing. The fish was still whole, the herbs weren't chopped. Maybe a few stocks, to make a finished sauce to order. I still believe in that philosophy. If you chop shallots, after two hours they smell of acid. So each order was apart, if an order for turbot soufflé came in, you had to fillet the turbot *à la minute,* cut the shallots, cut the tomatoes—everything done very fast. I think that's when I first started hearing my own voice in the lightness of his food.

A few years there and another phone call, and off I went to another three-star as *chef de partie* at Paul Bocuse. It was a dream I'd had for a long time, to work in his restaurant. He was one of the judges when I did my apprenticeship. The best cooking in France is regional cooking, and he defined it. It was classic but very influenced by Lyon.

Then I went to the total opposite, Eckhart Witzigmann at Aubergine, in Munich. I knew him from when he worked at La Napoule. He was even worse than Outhier; he posted the menu at four o'clock for seven-o'clock service. That's when we found out what we had to cook for that night's dinner. I was a sous-chef at Aubergine in 1979 when Outhier called me and said he was consulting for the Oriental hotels and asked me if I'd go be the chef at the hotel in Bangkok. I said, "What do you mean? I'm not a chef; I'm a sous-chef." I believe when you take a kitchen over, it's not just about you anymore. You have to know how to organize, you have to distribute dishes to different stations; costs are important. Even your language changes. As a sous-chef, my language was yes, no, and good morning. He called me back, and finally I said, "Okay, I'll go." I thought, "If I fail over there, I'll just pack my suitcases and come back."

I was twenty-three when I went to Thailand. I remember arriving in Bangkok. In those days you still walked off the plane and across the tarmac. There was an incredible mix of heat and smells like I'd never experienced before. I think I could already sense that this was going to be a life-changing place for me. I arrived at the hotel, and the first dish I had was *tum yam koong,* the traditional shrimp and lemongrass broth. Afterward they introduced me to the chef, and I asked him, "How do you make that soup?" It was a pot of water, lemongrass, lime leaves, a couple of shrimp, some fish sauce, lime juice, coriander. It was done in ten minutes with a pot of water. So my head went berserk, because I came from France, where everything was boiling for twenty hours and this was ten minutes and tap water and it was the best flavor I ever tasted. And that was it. I thought, "I'm throwing everything out and I'll start from scratch."

Of course, the wealthy clientele of the hotel wanted nothing to do with that kind of cooking. First of all, we lost most of our customers in the first months because we got rid of things like onion soup and steak au poivre. Then, when I started introducing dishes like foie gras with ginger and mango, they were horrified. They didn't want mangoes; those were sold on the street. They wanted apples because those had to be imported. It was very frustrating for me because I'd go to the market and see all these fantastic products but I couldn't use them. I tried to do a dish with pineapple once and they were like, "Whoa, pineapple, we give it away here!" But the princess of Thailand came one day, and the next day it was on the front page of the *Bangkok Post* and we were full every day after that. It was a small victory for me to put a little coriander here and there or some lemongrass or even a little ginger without saying it. And they were fine with it. I was very

275

satisfied that by the time I left, foie gras with mango and ginger was on the menu and a big seller.

I became something of a traveling chef, a specialist in opening restaurants. I went to Singapore, Hong Kong, Tokyo, Geneva, Portugal, and London. In 1986, I came to New York to open Lafayette, in the Drake Hotel. I was supposed to stay a year and move on to open something else in Chicago. But New York captured me, I loved the mix of the energy and the openness and the many cultures. The restaurant was fairly busy. Maybe thirty covers at lunch and forty for dinner. But when I went to an Italian restaurant and saw they were packed, I said to myself, "We're in Midtown, too, and we're half empty." I knew I needed to spice things up. I started going to Chinatown, and I said, "Wow, everything is here: lemongrass, lime leaves, ginger." I called Louis Outhier and I said I wanted to change things. He said, "Go for it, *mon p'tit,*" which is what he called me. My first dish was shrimp with carrot juice and Thai spices. It had cinnamon and nutmeg and cloves—a bit like a carrot cake. Spices can be so cleansing. I don't think people understood that. It's really the dish that marked a new beginning for the restaurant.

For ten years I'd been cooking somebody else's food. I was twenty-nine and I did not feel complete. I knew New York was open to something new. Gilbert Le Coze had opened Le Bernardin a few months before I arrived. I sensed it was time for me to try and do something myself. One of our best customers at Lafayette was Phil Suarez. One day he said to me, "When you want to open your own restaurant, give me a call. Here's my card." This was very New York style. He was a music producer; he did "Beat It." One day wandering around the Upper East Side, where I lived, I saw a sign of a place for lease. I called, and the owner said I could have it. I put down a ten-thousand-dollar deposit and then called Phil. We had lunch. He asked me what I needed to fix the place. I said, "I don't know, a hundred and fifty or two hundred thousand." He wrote me a check right there.

Then I went to school, to Hunter College. At the time they had a three-month crash course on how to open your own business. So I did my crash course, and we spent our last cent just as JoJo opened its doors. It was an immediate success. At the time, 250 restaurants were closing in New York every year. But something caught on about JoJo, and I was able to pay Phil back in six months. It was like downscaling Lafayette. It was the food I created at Lafayette for a third of the price. My dream had been to open one restaurant like André Soltner and spend the rest of my life there. But after a year, I looked in the mirror and I knew it was going to be different. JoJo is small; it's like a double-decker bus. I had so many ideas—one was for a Thai-French restaurant—and I went back to Phil and he said, "How much do you need?" He's been my partner ever since.

The first time I left JoJo for Vong, I knew it was the hardest thing for me. You lose twenty percent of something when you pass it on. If I give you a recipe, it's going to be there minus twenty percent. Same thing if someone gives one to me. Today we have sixteen restaurants in three continents and thirty-two hundred employees. My role is to close that gap to ten percent, and five percent, and finally zero percent, and make it as if I'm in all of them. I'm in touch with the restaurants every day. I take the chefs to Shanghai or somewhere else exciting; I take them out of their context. And there is an exchange. I give them twenty percent, but they give me twenty percent, too. My greatest challenge is not to disappoint people. I'm not just talking about customers. When we closed V Steakhouse, I felt I had disappointed the team who had put their heart into it. Usually things don't get to that point; the beautiful thing in this business is that whatever is broken for lunch is fixed for dinner.

I spend one week a month out of New York. I go to the office every morning. I think it's important when you open a business to be behind the business. If the numbers don't work, the business doesn't work. Still I need to spend at least six hours a day in the kitchen; it's my ego peel. I also think it's crucial to stay engaged in the restaurants at the level of ingredients. At the moment I'm really excited by fresh herbs I get in China that we usually know as dry. Say, fresh aniseed or fresh coriander seed. For a French chef, dry coriander seed is associated with the *à la grecque* style of cooking vegetables, and it really excites me to think of it used fresh in certain dishes. Despite all the restaurants, cooking has never lost its ability to be an expression for me. At Jean-Georges we do a sea trout sashimi with trout eggs and lemon froth and horseradish with a crispy skin that is a perfect balance of who I am: raw, crunchy, a little sour, maybe a little sweet as well.

My greatest luxury is silence. When you talk to people all day long I feel it's very important. I don't listen to music. I have driven in New York for fifteen years and I like to drive around in a car that's just big enough to frighten the cabs and take in the city. I have three children, and my son is going to go into the business, but I never would have told him he had to. Getting three Michelin stars for Jean-Georges was very special for me. For the first seven years of my professional life I worked in three-stars. I escaped them when I came to America, but they followed me here. I suppose I can say it took me thirty-three years to get three stars. The first person I called was Louis Outhier. He really was my mentor in how to keep the level. How to keep the level—that's what it's about. It's a challenge every day to keep the standard. I guess I'm part of the mafia now.